Making Faces, *Playing God*

THOMAS MORAWETZ

Making Faces

Playing God

Identity

and the Art of

Transformational

Makeup

 University of Texas Press, Austin

Copyright © 2001 by the University of Texas Press

All rights reserved
Printed in China
First edition, 2001

Requests for permission to reproduce material from this work
should be sent to Permissions, University of Texas Press, Box
7819, Austin, TX 78713-7819.

⊚ The paper used in this book meets the minimum require-
ments of ANSI/NISO Z39.48-1992 (R1997) (Permanence of
Paper).

Library of Congress Cataloging-in-Publication Data

Morawetz, Thomas, 1942–

Making faces, playing God : identity and the art of transformational makeup / Thomas Morawetz.
     p.   cm.
ISBN 0-292-75246-6 (alk. paper)—ISBN 0-292-75247-4 (pbk. :
alk. paper)
1. Theatrical makeup.   2. Impersonation.   3. Self-perception.
I. Title.

PN2068.M59 2001
792'.027—DC21   00-064846

Frontispiece: Alien from *Babylon 5*. Makeup by John Vulich/
Optic Nerve.

For Herb and Margie Morris,
and for Julian Offsay,
with gratitude

Contents

Acknowledgments

Transformational makeup projects are typically collaborative. Design and sculpture, production of prosthetic appliances, and the application of the makeup to the actor involve teams of artists. For the most part, it is impossible to identify and acknowledge all of the craftspersons who make essential contributions. I have generally attributed each makeup project to the studio that produced it. Only in a few cases has it been possible to discover and list the hands-on artists.

Many makeup artists and staff members of makeup studios were generous with information and time, and their help was indispensable. I am grateful to Rick Baker, Gabe Bartalos, Todd Bates, Howard Berger, Brian Blair, Rick Bongiovanni, Donovan Brown, Norman Bryn, Michele Burke, John Caglione, Jr., John Chambers, Bill Corso, Fionagh Cush, John Dods, Dave Dupuis, Joe Fordham, Ed French, Carl Fullerton, Greg Funk, Jerry Gergely, Alec Gillis, Alan Gray, Robert Hall, Kevin Haney, Joel Harlow, Steve Johnson, Barry Koper, Steve LaPorte, Jeff Lewis, Toby Lindala, Brad Look, Göran Lundström, Jerry Macaluso, Marta Manus, Todd Masters, Todd McIntosh, Matthew Mungle, Kari Murillo, Ve Neill, Bob Newton, Scott Patton, Michael Pearce, Jerry Quist, James Rohland, Gordon Smith, Richard Snell, Maurice Stein, Pierre-Olivier Thévènin, John Vulich, Chad Washam, John Weldy, Jr., Michael Westmore, Tom Woodruff, Jr., Olivier Xavier, and Kevin Yagher. Of these, I owe special debts to Gabe Bartalos, Kevin Haney, Steve Johnson, Todd Masters, Todd McIntosh, Matthew Mungle, Maurice Stein, and John Vulich for allowing me frequent and unstinting access to their archives and their world.

I had the pleasure of discussing their work as aliens and monsters with several actors. I am indebted to Wayne Alexander, Keith Campbell, Tom Choate, Josh Patton, Eric Pierpoint, T. Ryder Smith, Kim Strauss, Lee Whitaker, and Eric

Zivot. I am also grateful to Tony Mendez for talking with me about using his disguise expertise for the CIA.

David Culmer, James Scrimgeour, and Carol Weisbrod all read the manuscript and all made creative and insightful suggestions. James Scrimgeour also helped cheerfully with the thankless task of soliciting permissions to use photos. It would not have been possible to reproduce and organize those photos without the skills of Jeff Day at Camera City and Photo in Los Angeles and Dave Farrington at Zacher's in West Hartford, Connecticut.

Introduction

Zeus, the most powerful of Greek gods, had the ability to transform himself—into a bull, into a mortal. Even lesser gods were able to change their physical nature; it was the defining characteristic of Proteus.

Mortals, however, are doomed to inhabit one body with constant features. Bodies change, but changes tend to be gradual as we grow up and age, and the changes are hardly magical. But people have always fought these limits and tried to go beyond them. Alterations—tattoos, body piercings, and surgical reconstruction—have been part of every culture and are once more popular in ours. Festivals that seduce celebrants into assuming new identities—carnivals, Halloween—are universal. Although part of the purpose of self-change is decoration, enhancement, or beauty, the deeper and more radical purpose is transformation.

This book is about a group of artist-magicians who practice the art of transformation. Their talent and their job is the creation of new beings, human and almost human, and they succeed in doing so with disconcerting completeness. Their work shares many features with other artistic traditions; they are artists in the fullest sense. Their talent lies in sculpting and painting, but their material is not canvas or stone but rubber or other materials that have the character of near-flesh. Like architects, their designs are executed by teams of craftsmen and engineers and involve daunting technological challenges. Like performance artists, their work is not static, but ephemeral and animated. Like every other art, theirs is an art that conceals art; it works its magic only because it fools us into accepting what is created as a new and real entity.

What is unique about these artists is that their raw material includes not steel, glass, and bricks, not canvas and oil paint, but living, breathing human beings.

While there is very little shock value in comparing an empty canvas with a painting, or a warehouse of steel and glass with a finished building, there is a world of wonder in comparing the model with the wholly new being he or she has become. When the transformation works, we confront a person with a new life and history. We face a moribund beach bum in whose face we read a lifetime of hardship. Or a nearly human demon that reanimates the hellfire of medieval art. Or an ambassador from an otherworldly civilization that has followed its own independent but discernible course of evolution.

For most of these makeup artists, transformational makeup is only a small part of their bag of skills and tricks. Their talents extend to all kinds of horror effects, to the creation of animatronic creatures and body parts, to electronic and computer-based transformations, and so on. But most of these effects are designed to fool only the movie camera and not the eye. On the other hand, our main focus in this book is on the magical creation of freestanding new persons with whom one can shake hands, have lunch, and go for a walk.

The projects discussed in this book came about under varied circumstances. Some are demonstration makeups in which the artist tested the limits of his skills. Others were created as trials that never made it to the finished film. Still others are familiar successes, involving superstars and box office recognition.

The projects themselves are also dizzyingly varied. They include the step-by-step transformation of Tim Allen into Santa Claus, the creation of a universe of alien civilizations, the summoning of medieval demons, the reincarnation of historical figures, and triumphs of extreme aging.

For this kind of artistry, pictures are not just worth a thousand words; they are beyond worth. They are magical twice over. They allow us to savor in detail the artists' triumphs, to compare their aims with their successes. And they allow us to witness the transformation and see how persons are reinvented. The pictures in this book are unique in trying to do justice to the magic. But words are also needed—not just to tell the stories of the makeups but to raise tantalizing questions about the nature of acting, the relationship of appearance and identity, and the transcendence of self implicit in transformation.

For some curmudgeons, these stories are only about persons wearing pieces of rubber, just as paintings are only canvases with bits of pigment. For them, acting always comes "from inside" and needs no special effects. For them, transformation is not a daring way to challenge our limits, to challenge mortality. This book is for everyone else.

Part 1

The Culture and Art of Transformation

Chapter 1

The
Significance and
Invention of Faces

A world in which no person *recognizes* anyone else.
The main activity of these people would be
to convince each other *that they are who they are.*

ELIAS CANETTI, *The Human Province*

Giving Faces the Recognition They Deserve

Don't underestimate faces. It matters that our faces are unique and make for easy recognition. Imagine a world in which we are all cloned from five or twenty different models (like cars), a world in which each of us is visually identical to millions of others. In that world, we could tell strangers from friends or lovers only by inspecting identity cards or other hidden marks of identity. In such a world, intimacy and friendship—social life, family life, business life as we know them—could no longer exist in the ways they do. In important ways we would no longer be human. The possibility of compromising our uniqueness, the mere fantasy of having a double, threatens our identity. Don't twins, familiar as they may be, always seem a bit unsettling?

For unique identifiability, faces matter more than bodies. A picture of a person is generally a picture of his or her face. Imagine trying to recognize others by inspecting their thumbs or ankles. However much we differ in our ability to remember faces, we are all finely attuned to noticing and recalling persons we have met. Our powers go well beyond anything we can express in words. We know that we can recognize Smith, and we know equally well that we can never describe what makes his appearance unique. And our powers of recognition go beyond our powers of imaginative recall. We know that we can recognize Jones even if we are not sure whether he still has his mustache and still wears glasses.

Easy recognizability, for all the benefits it makes possible, has its drawbacks. We are generally held responsible for the things we do. Anonymity, as countless authors, movie stars, and malefactors have found, is hard to contrive and maintain. Our identity is melded with our personal history. That history is a public and social artifact; we have little power to change it in retrospect although we have some control over its creation in the first place.

Recognizability is only one aspect, one consequence of having a face. Other consequences relate to the nature of one's face, visible to strangers and familiars alike. Poets and psychologists claim to believe that one's character is written on one's face. Orwell said that "at fifty, everyone has the face he deserves." Perhaps. Or perhaps the opposite is true, and our faces remain masks that conceal as much as they reveal about our true natures, if there is such a thing as a "true nature." And perhaps faces are neither mirrors of the soul nor masks, but partly one and partly the other, expressing and concealing our nature to different audiences at different times. Perhaps we all use our faces to fool at least some of the people some of the time. Perhaps we are transparent to some observers and opaque to others.

In any case, reading faces is an activity that gives photography and portraiture much of their raison d'être. Faces, in fact, are as much a vehicle of communication as words, and both faces and words can lie. Moreover, what we express with our faces is not necessarily intentional or within our control. Even when faces do not lie, they can mislead, and they can betray.

It is hard, if not impossible, to tell where expression ends and the "natural" disposition of our features begins. Expression is ephemeral, but the configuration of features is fixed, and what we convey to others is an amalgam of both. Expression, moreover, may be inadvertent. We differ enormously in our ability to control and manipulate the messages, liminal and subliminal, that we send.

In all these ways, faces matter insofar as they are natural, not artificial. Identifying persons and holding them responsible for what they do depends on the fact that they have one and only one unique and natural face for life. The ways in which we refer to the use and abuse of responsibility presuppose the identification of the person with his or her face. We talk about "bare-faced lies" and refer to shame that reaches the point of annihilation as "losing face." All contacts between ourselves and the world outside us are called "interface."

Of course, our "natural" faces are not altogether natural. Certain kinds of artifice are common, generally nondeceptive, and consistent with having a uniquely recognizable face. In many contexts cosmetic enhancement is the norm, as much to be expected as wearing clothes. Even cosmetic surgery, a more radical and permanent change, usually modifies what nature has bestowed but leaves one recognizable.

It follows that one of the most unnerving and subversive fantasies we can have is that of not being able to trust the constancy and the naturalness, and thus the recognizability, of faces. Such fantasies take many forms. Consider three. The most virulent and unsettling—and a staple of early horror and science fiction—has one's own face change uncontrollably and unpredictably. Staring in the mirror for reassurance, one sees a werewolf, Mr. Hyde, a large cockroach, or at least an utter stranger glaring back. A vampire finds no reflection at all. In all such cases, one's place in the world is put into jeopardy.

A second fantasy, less dire, less shattering, has one able to change appearance, even shape, at will. This differs from the first fantasy because one has control. Dr. Jekyll gains control not of Mr. Hyde's actions but of his access to his other self, his other face. The ancient gods—Jupiter, Venus—and even lesser gods like Proteus could opt to assume mortal guises. (A variant story is that of optional invisibility—but being invisible has disadvantages: more substantial beings are likely to run into you and be suspicious when doors and chairs seem to move of their own accord.) Metamorphosis at will liberates one from attribution and responsibility. It becomes the necessary means, the perfect means, for committing and getting away with illicit action.

A third fantasy, neither as alarming as the first nor as liberating as the second, is that others have the power to change faces at will, at random. Here the identity of others, not of oneself, becomes problematic, and again connections to the world, trust, and constancy are all jeopardized. In vesting others with the power of metamorphosis, this fantasy erases the border between nature and artifice. In Chapter 2, I explore the many ways in which all three kinds of fantasy are (and have always been) staples of popular culture.

Obviously, our ability to function in life—intimate life, social life, business life—depends on our ability to put such fantasies aside, to be sure they are nothing but fantasies. Faces and identities, we are content to assume, really are natural, really are fixed by God or at least by our genes. For the most part, then, experience as personal recognition can be trusted. Or can it?

Making and Remaking Faces: The Arts of God and Man

Movies sometimes demand faces that do not appear in nature. Aliens from other planets are, as yet, in short supply—and so human actors have to be reconfigured as aliens. Benign-looking actors may have to appear demonic. A script may call for an actor to follow the trajectory from youth to extreme age, to gain hundreds of pounds, or to be disfigured. A movie may involve Napoleon, Winston Churchill, Abraham Lincoln, or Mark Twain—and none of them is available to play himself. A movie may even be about the very process of disguise, of transforming oneself in order to commit or investigate crime.

Makeup artists have refined the art of creating faces. At their very best they mimic what God or genes-as-nature are able to do: create artificial faces that do just about everything that natural faces do and thus convince us they are natural. Both in repose and in movement, they express identity. They can be "read" to evoke a personal history, a set of dispositions and propensities, a spectrum of feelings and expectations. We can be fooled to the extent that artifice takes over our response. Even when we may know that we are confronted with a convincing false face rather than a real one, we may experience—viscerally and emotionally—the face as real and the actor as provisionally lost within the makeup.

Portraits affect our emotions and thoughts in similar ways, but the subjects of portraits stay put within their frames, have two dimensions, and are not animated with the expressive range of real faces. Our transactions with portraits are therefore "safe"; we run no risk of confusing them with real persons. And the creation of portraits, fascinating as it may be, is comparatively simple. The raw material is blank canvas rather than the embodied, expressive flesh of a living being.

The collaboration between the makeup artist and the actor is also a kind of performance art. It is ephemeral: the created being exists briefly, surviving only to be recorded on film or tape. But while it exists, the creation has its own characteristics, its personality, its relationships and idiosyncracies.

All art conceals art. The makeup artist is no more or less an artist by virtue of the fact that success depends on fooling us, on surreptitiously counterfeiting the role of God or nature. Paintings must distract us from thinking of them as pigment and canvas. Music must be thought of as something more than and other than coincident vibrations evoked by metal, wood, and fiber. Works of architecture must conceal their complexity behind a veneer of order and coherence. Each translates artifice into an experience that mimics what nature is or what ideally it should be. The makeup artist as crafter of faces does no less.

The art of the makeup artist, moreover, is fiendishly difficult. The ideal, I think, is not simply to replicate real faces—any more than the ideal of a sculptor is to mimic as closely as possible an actual person, or horse, or tree. (If that were so, plaster casts of real objects would rival the work of sculptors.) Rather, the ideal is to evoke the feelings, attitudes, and responses that only the most expressive faces call forth. Created faces can do this only if they are realistic to the point of seducing us to suspend disbelief, to lose sight of the person who is the raw material, to see the actor as subverted into the work of art. We confront a face that mirrors both a credible person and the essence of the demonic, or a recognizable being that reflects the character and evolutionary history of an alien race, or a simulacrum of Harry Truman that is also somehow the essence of Truman.

What makes the art daunting is not merely, not primarily, the expressive task. Rather, it is the technical challenge, the recalcitrance of the materials. It is nearly impossible to make rubber (prosthetic appliances) look and act like flesh. The process of creating prosthetic pieces is complex, exacting, and unforgiving. The ideal is often betrayed by the fact that rubber reflects light differently from flesh. We forget that skin is translucent; we are so accustomed to seeing its depths and its layers that we are only aware of what's missing and what's artificial when masks or crude cosmetics give themselves away. Even when rubber appliances give the subtle illusion of depth, they rarely move, crease, fold, dimple in the ways of flesh. None of this means that the goal is impossible, quixotic. It does mean that, even before the expressive challenge is addressed, the practical and technical demands of this kind of art leave no margin for error. It also means that photos, such as the ones displayed here, tell a skewed part of the artist's story, just as photos of sculpture or architecture present their subjects more adequately than words but give us a mere echo of immediate experience. Moreover, photos allow the artist to control lighting and ignore the challenge of movement and animation. The artist's success along these dimensions must be taken on faith.

The Arts of the Makeup Artist

This book's story about the art of makeup artists identifies and explores a neglected art form, and it captures only a slice of the artists' craft and business. Most makeup artists are occupied with beautification or with accommodating the distorting effects of cameras and film. A distinct and discrete minority specializes in so-called special effects makeup. Transformational character makeup is part of their bag of tricks, but most often their job is to devise other kinds of special effects.

Most moviegoers know these artists best as midwives of horror and gore. In the late 1960s and early 1970s the movie industry changed our expectations about staging violence. Such movies as *Bonnie and Clyde* and *The Godfather* series achieved new levels of realism, and ever since directors of crime and disaster movies have been raising the stakes for recreating mayhem and violent death.

A different growth industry within special effects makeup responds to the demands of science fiction and fantasy. Increasingly, such movies use creations that are not variations of the human form or not plausibly reconfigurations of the human face. Paradoxically, this too is an advance in realism, tracking the insight that there is no reason to assume that monsters and extraterrestrial beings should be expected to look like men in masks and rubber suits. More than any other movies, the original *Star Wars* trilogy revolutionized our expectations about the realistic evocation of the unreal.

In these contexts, the makeup artist's bag of tricks has come to include animatronics and computer manipulation of characters. The former involves creatures that are motor-driven constructions of metal and plastic, clothed in rubber and fur to look and behave like animals, insects, monsters, or disembodied body parts. Computer-based metamorphoses, used pioneeringly in *Terminator 2: Judgment Day,* allow human actors to appear to dissolve, to become metal or liquid, and to fly apart into pieces. What is distinctive in these uses of new technology is that they exist for the sake of the camera and produce an image that cannot exist in reality. The magic and illusion occur only when the cables and operators that run the animatronic creature are blocked out, and only when the computer produces a series of pictures that allow a man to appear to change form into a wolf.

By contrast, the technology that allows makeup artists to sculpt faces and, God-like, create new persons is relatively rudimentary and has been around for much of the century. Like the technology of sculpture and painting, it has evolved slowly. Also, like those other arts, its creations have an existence apart from the camera. This particular Abe Lincoln or Harry Truman who happens to be around in the 1990s, this extraterrestrial gentleman with no nose and one eye, and this young actor newly aged and to all intents and purposes inhabiting his eighties are all beings we can encounter, appraise, and interact with in real space and time, much as we can take into our lives the sculptures, paintings, and buildings that are the fruits of other arts. To be sure, they are impermanent and ephemeral, artificial faces that can be worn, at most, for about a day at a time. In this ephemeral quality, this link with performance, they are comparable to the arts of dance and music.

In other words, the makeup artist's art bridges the skills of fine arts, engineering, and computer technology—and the projects in all their diversity can be sorted into categories. Some jobs, those that involve the invention of character through the creation of faces, make lavish demands on artistic skills such as sculpture and painting, but are indisputably low tech. Other jobs, those that involve animatronic and computer-based camera illusions, may begin on the drawing board but are heavily dependent on technology. In concentrating on makeup artists as inventors of character and as reinventors of real faces, this book focuses on the former.

In all fields there are generalists and specialists, and specialists are particularly dependent on market demand for the special genius. Some makeup artists have absorbed the various new technologies to maintain studios-of-all-trades. Rick Baker (Cinovation Studios), Alec Gillis and Tom Woodruff Jr. (ADI), Steve Johnson (XFX), John Vulich (Optic Nerve), Greg Nicotero and Howard Berger (KNB), Todd Masters, and Stan Winston run studios that take on many kinds of projects—creatures of fantasy, animatronic animals and insects, horror effects, and so on. Other makeup artists of great skill, among them Kevin Haney, Matthew Mungle, and Carl Fullerton remain purists, refining the art of transformational character makeup and expanding its scope.

Both specialists and generalists tend to see character makeup, face creation of the kind celebrated in this book, as their highest challenge and greatest achievement. As Tom Woodruff Jr. suggested in an interview, technologies of all kinds are the means, but the invention of character is always the end. Most of these artists cherish the relatively rare projects that require the subtle reinvention of faces—aging, recreating historical characters, or reinventing actors as aliens and demons.

Even when such jobs exist, time and money can constrain artistic craft. Given the practical commercial limits of moviemaking, makeup artists are more likely to see themselves as guns-for-hire than as pure artists. The same compromises, of course, shape the lives of architects, composers, and many writers. But we all can cite the rare architect or composer who has achieved the renown and clout to be independent, to chase his or her muse at full throttle. Circumstances and the ephemeral character of their output have, for the most part, denied makeup artists that status.

As a result, their best art is often secret, or at least little known. Some of the very best character makeups, ones that are disturbingly expressive and convincing, are often created solely for the artist's portfolio. Or they may be projects that die on the cutting room floor. Or they may appear in unreleased movies, or movies with vanishingly limited distribution. Most of the startling and disconcerting creations in this book will in fact be unfamiliar . . . but hardly all. Rick Baker's work on Eddie Murphy for *Coming to America* and *The Nutty Professor,* and some of Mike Westmore's aliens for various *Star Trek* series are known to millions and are essential factors in the success of the shows themselves.

Seeing Faces as Art

Art, for the most part, is dyadic, transactions between artists and their audiences. We no longer think of the artist as active and the audience as passive. Informed by postmodernism, we appreciate the active, constructive role of the reader, viewer, or listener. Postmodernism also invites us to see the artist or creator as one among many audiences of the work. The artist's own reading or interpretation is not necessarily definitive or even privileged. Rather, the work of art is sent into the world to fend for itself, to acquire a life and a history, to be understood, interpreted, and used.

The characters and inventions in this book stand on their own. The thoughts and intentions of the makeup artists are of endless interest, but they are not determinative of our response. And my responses, as one bemused observer, are not yours. These pictures, depicting these creatures, are not worth a thousand or a million words; they are incommensurable with words.

But any awareness of makeup artists' thoughts and intentions is especially paradoxical when their aim is to tease us into seeing the work as natural. Even if all artists are illusionists, and even if all art conceals art, makeup artists do so in a special way. However we may be fooled by other kinds of art, we are not likely to see buildings or sculptures as natural growths or to mistake symphonies for the play of the winds. But successful makeup artists must conceal not only their models but also their role as creator. Success depends on our being whipsawed between a subliminal awareness of artifice and an emotional response that contradicts and dispels that awareness. This fact underlines both the magnitude of the makeup artists' challenge and the unsettling effects of their art.

The inventions of makeup artists are different from other arts in yet a different way, since they presuppose a relationship that is in fact triadic. The third player is the person who both wears and is the work of art. The work of art is and is not his face, is and is not her person. This triadic relationship, involving the indispensable role of the actor or model, is unlike other arts, even those in which performance is essential. It is, for example, unlike music where the indispensable third partner is the interpreter, but where the music exists to be interpreted by indefinitely many interpreters. The actor, like the makeup artist, collaborates in the creation of character and physiognomy. Like the viewer, the actor is a witness, in this case a witness to his or her own transformation. But unlike both the makeup artist and the viewer, the actor also embodies and becomes the work of art, animating it and giving it life.

Transformational makeup forces us to revisit traditional questions about the art of acting, in particular about the relationship of the actor to his roles. Arguably, character makeup perfects the actor's task by allowing him to subvert his identity completely, to lose himself in the role and be unrecognizable to others. In a contrasting view, the most perfect acting dispenses with props and crutches, with costumes and cosmetics, and creates illusion with resources that come from "inside" the actor.

Both views are seductive but simplistic. Acting is not reducible to either internal or external elements, and it is not a matter of merely losing oneself or fooling others. It is, if anything, a dialectical process of self-discovery through discovering the nature and character of other characters. In different ways the audience, as well as the actor, is transformed through such a process. For both actor and audience, transformational character makeup can heighten the distance between the actor and the artificial, created being he or she becomes, and at the same time, paradoxically, lead us to ponder their identity. In this sense it gives added dimensions to the art of acting and its effects, deepening its mysteries. At the end of Chapter 2, we will revisit the transformational aspects of acting.

However fascinating it may be, the makeup artist's magic (the art of transforming faces) may be dismissed as a peripheral and utilitarian art, as merely making possible certain kinds of theatrical effects and cinematic illusions. The next two chapters defend a broader view of the cultural, artistic, and psychological importance of transformation. To take the makeup artist's creations as artistic ends in themselves is, as we will see, to be moved and disturbed in various ways. To consider the reality of false faces excites questions about identity, appearance, recognition, and transformation that are familiarly troubling exercises of imagination.

Chapter 2 argues that the preoccupations about identity, self-knowledge, and change evoked by these artifacts are some of the same preoccupations that inform much that is fascinating in philosophy, psychology, religion, and anthropology. Philosophers worry about the links between the sense of personal identity and the determinateness of our bodies. Psychologists examine the ways in which self-knowledge and self-acceptance are tied to the appearance we present to the world, the way we appear to ourselves as well as others. Moreover, to understand culture is in part to confront the interest of every society in masks, carnival, and plays in which actors adopt false personae. At the heart of all these concerns are the emotions and fears involved in contemplating our own identity—its malleability, its ephemeral nature—and the reality of our own masks. These issues take us into some of the richest thickets of academic debate.

Chapter 2

The Culture of Transformation

Scully: Looking like someone else, Mulder,
and being someone else are completely different things.
Mulder: Maybe it's not. Everybody else would treat you like you
were someone else; ultimately maybe it's other people's
reactions to us that make us what we are.

X-Files, "SMALL POTATOES"

Introduction: Through the Looking Glass

Consider mirrors. You check mirrors for information and reassurance, and you do so because you are not really sure what you will see. And you may well be surprised by the leaf of spinach caught between your teeth or the smudge of soot on your nose.

But you are quite certain you will not learn from the mirror that you have two heads, changed gender, or aged fifty years since this morning. That is the stuff of science fiction. For the most part, we know where experience ends and imagination begins.

How do we distinguish the domain of experience from the domain of imagination? A first response is that experience follows rules but imagination is free. It is easy to think that following the rules of experience is mandated by what we call the laws of physics, biology, psychology, and other sciences, while using imagination is volitional and unbounded.

But it is also possible to question both parts of that claim. Some philosophers argue that what we call experience is not simply *given* but socially constructed. Experience is not just *what happens* (in accord with scientific laws) but is determined by our expectations and our collective ways of thinking, for example by the practices and habits embedded in language. Different cultures and different societies will have different ground rules for what counts as experience.

Imagination, on the other hand, may not be free but may have its own rules. Perhaps we are no freer to abstain from certain flights of imagination than we are free to abstain from obeying gravity. To talk about universal forms of imagination is not at all a paradox. Popular psychologists tell us, unsurprisingly, that sexual fantasies fall into common and predictable categories. On a more abstract plane, the influential Swiss psychologist Carl Jung and his disciple Joseph Campbell claimed to derive influential theories of human nature from the universal myths that animate cultural imagination.

This book celebrates one profound and universal dimension of imagination. It argues that a significant part of the work of imagination plays variations on our awareness that we are given one unique and determinate face and body and, in more general terms, one identity. This awareness is our common predicament as self-conscious persons. It cuts across cultures and across time. What are the ways in which we cope with it both as individuals and as cultures?

The play of imagination with the themes of identity, appearance, recognizability, physical determinateness, and transformation runs across our cultural practices. Philosophy, religion, psychology, cultural anthropology, and the theory and practice of acting—all of these are fields in which abstract and empirical scholarship sometimes mask, sometimes reveal the ways in which our imagination is seduced by the mysteries of identity and the possibilities of transformation.

Philosophy and Religion: On Being Mindful of Bodies

Skeptical philosophy sits at the intersection of experience and imagination. It tells us that we are insufficiently astonished by the regularity of experience. Skeptics express awe over the facts that we can distinguish wakefulness from dreaming, that we can generally trust our memories, and that objects continue to behave in familiar and predictable ways. The skeptic's point is that the learned processes of experience express *how* experience works—but ultimately they can never tell us *why*. Nothing can justify its regularity. We may come to think that we are favored by experience in this way, that regularity is a gift. To function at all in the familiar world is to reap the benefit of that gift. (The philosopher Ludwig Wittgenstein asks whether "we could stay in the saddle however much the facts might buck?" He makes us wonder how much, or how little, irregularity it would take—objects suddenly liquefying, friends turning into reptiles—for us to stop making judgments at all.)

One such gift, one aspect of the regularity of experience, is the stability of self-awareness and self-knowledge. Awareness of self has many components. Some are simply physical. We know and can describe all sorts of personal features, from our height and weight to scars, the size of our noses, and the shape of our fingernails. And we can safely assume that these features will remain stable or change gradually. Other components are mental and emotional. We retain memories and can summon them, and we generally know what we like, what we abhor, what amuses us, what bores us, and what we fear. Still other components are interpersonal. We take for granted that others will recognize us and that we will for the most part be able to anticipate and understand what they say and do.

The skeptical philosopher gains leverage on our imagination by challenging (deconstructing) this web of assumptions. Skeptical suggestions are the stuff of science fiction or horror. Imagine looking in the mirror and confronting a flamingo or a leopard. You nod or blink, and the leopard blinks back. Or imagine looking in the mirror and finding that you have changed race overnight, or simply grown fangs. In this story, you have continuous memory and consciousness but cannot explain your physical change. Or imagine a different story, that you recognize yourself in the mirror but that friends and lovers claim you are a stranger, while strangers claim you are their friend, that they've known you all their lives.

The skeptic's point is that identity is fragile. The stability of experience and self-awareness is, for all we can justify or explain, a happy coincidence. The skeptic asks what we would say about identity if our minds, with memories and knowledge intact, were transplanted to another body. And what could we say if our body continued to exist but was reusable, was used by a newly implanted mind? The physical self that others continue to recognize, now inhabited with a transferred consciousness, might seem to them simply afflicted with amnesia.

The lessons of the skeptic are many. At one level, the questions simply challenge the coherence of the concepts of identity and self. They are hardly impervious to doubt. In our hypotheses, where bodily continuity is severed from continuity of consciousness and memory, what is the stable self, the continuing identity? Who am I?

In practice, we usually can put aside the skeptic's questions by bracketing them as mere possibility. (Such questions *do* come up, for example, with Alzheimer's patients. At what point does their failing sense of self imply that they have lost identity as well, that they are no longer "the same person"?) As long as our friends and enemies continue to recognize us, our mirrors reflect no profound metamorphoses, and our memories are constant, we can refer to this package as the self. Only when circumstances collapse and the skeptic's science fiction–like hypotheses are realized must we go back to the concept factory and retool our notion of identity.

But at a second level the skeptic's insight is not just a tantalizing possibility, and it is deeply unsettling. Once we are forced to imagine these nightmares, can we be the same again? Once we see that identity is fragile, can we disregard and dismiss the disturbing implications of these imaginings?

Perhaps we can, if we've eaten a good meal and had a good night's sleep. (The eighteenth-century philosopher David Hume, who gave us clear accounts of skepticism, remarked that drinking and gambling with friends was the best antidote to skeptical doubts.) But what affects us, imaginatively and emotionally, about the skeptic's nightmares is their paradoxical impact: once joined, they are as liberating and inspiriting as they are fearsome. The ripple effect of the skeptic's questions is to unleash imagination in a way that makes familiar aspects of personal identity problematic and troubling.

One aspect is mortality. The one boringly familiar body we face in the mirror daily is one, as we know too well, that will age and die. The reassuring certainty that we will never have to confront a different face is also the disconcerting knowledge that we will never be able to escape this body with its infirmities and its fate. The skeptic's nightmare, the possibility of one consciousness migrating to different bodies, is also a glimpse of immortality and transcendence.

A second aspect is choice. Staying young is just one of many options denied us. We can choose our clothes but not our race or height. Nor can we choose our memories or, for the most part, our temperament. The skeptic invites us to see this predicament not merely as given, but also as problematic. He foists alternatives on us. We can ask, indeed we can hardly avoid asking, what it would be like to inhabit bodies radically different from our own. And we can ask the different question of what it would be like to have a choice in the matter, to be able to select from a menu of options what we see in the mirror and what others see when they meet us.

This fantasy of choice has even more seductive implications. It offers the option of relaxing, even leaving behind, the noose of personal responsibility. Retaining one's consciousness and memories while choosing a new face and body is not merely a matter of esthetics, a matter of possibly trading ordinariness for beauty. It is also a matter of morality. We are made responsible for what we do to the extent that others can identify us and *hold* us responsible. Here the skeptic's ideas allow us to sever our own sense of personal responsibility, which has nothing to do with being recognizable to others, from the social and legal experience of being held responsible, which has everything to do with recognition. To move from recognizability to anonymity is to leave blame and censure behind.

What is the relation between a personal sense of moral responsibility—and the uncomfortable emotions of shame and guilt which shape it—and the experience of being blamed? Psychologists argue persuasively that personal experience depends on what occurs *inter*personally. Unless one is taught to sort behavior into the permissible and impermissible, and is then held responsible and blameworthy in the face of shared rules, the interior aspect (the moral emotions) cannot flower. Even if we are born with the capacity for shame, guilt, and empathy, the capacity will not be realized unless we are socialized through practice and training.

If this is so and if reidentifiability is the lynchpin of being held responsible, then the skeptic's hypotheses have moral implications. It is not merely the case that a person who is capable of transformation, by avoiding identification, also avoids blame and punishment. (This accounts for the popularity of ski masks among terrorists and criminals. They are not just a fashion statement.) But if we hypothesize, in mythology or science fiction perhaps, a quicksilver Protean child who, from its first moment, is capable of assuming different physical appearances at will, that child will be incapable of learning morality. For her, evasion is just too easy.

In mythology and many religions, the gods are much like this Protean child. They are able to change their form and appearance at will, and they need never assume a fixed form. This explains why the morality of gods—in myths, for example—is so problematic and why their acts can seem so capricious. Because physical recognizability is not an essential part of their nature, neither are blame and responsibility. To act mercifully or benignly toward mortals is at best their gift and their indulgence, never their responsibility.

If the gods in myth and religion cannot be held morally responsible, the interactions of men and gods demonstrate the human preoccupation with trying to overcome these limits. In this respect, the relationship of individuals and God in Christianity is especially poignant. In the Old Testament, persons are warned against making and worshiping physical representations of God. It is a form of sin to see God embodied, to vest God with a fixed physical identity. In the New Testament, God becomes embodied in Christ and thus becomes capable of caring, suffering, and dying. The determinateness of human form makes possible moral mediation between God and persons.

Dealings with the unembodied God of the Old Testament are problematic. One implication of the story of the Tower of Babel is that language is a tool of human societies, of mortal beings, but that human individuals and God lack a common language. Analogously, Old Testament theology is much preoccupied with trying to explain how a God that is omnipotent—formless or capable of endless transformation—can also be a merciful God. The Gnostics suggested that such a God may be indifferent to human suffering and that altruism and mercy are ideas relevant only to relations among embodied beings with fixed identities.

Comparing the situations of persons with faces and social identities firmly in place with the gods of myth and religion allows us to raise questions about freedom as well as responsibility. To be able to assume and change faces at will exempts us from being identified and thus, we suppose, from being held responsible. This allows us, in consequence, the freedom of gods, the freedom to do whatever we want.

But note how strange and *unhuman* a kind of freedom this is. As a political notion, freedom involves acting with impunity. More generally, it means having choices about acting-and-refraining in a context in which such choices are allowed and respected. It is, as Daniel Dennett suggests, a kind of elbow room. But elbow room (or political freedom) makes sense only in a context in which there are *some* rules. If everything is permitted because there are no rules and no transgressions, then it is also the case that *nothing* is permitted (because there are no rules).

The freedom of the gods lures us only because we see it—in human terms and therefore mistakenly—as transgression. Maybe we are all criminals at heart, wanting to break the rules that others follow, and transformation (as disguise) may sometimes allow us to get away with just that. But this cannot be the gods' experience of freedom. For them there are in principle no rules to transgress and no judicial bodies to hold them liable.

Here again, fantasies inspired by philosophical skeptics lead to conflicting responses. What if we suffered unpredictable and radical physical transformation? Alternatively, what if we had the power to control that process? The horrors of the first possibility, and the tantalizing opportunities of the second, show the skeptic's power to inflame imagination. Mortality, responsibility, and freedom are not mere political and social concepts but the basic stuff of experience and imagination, of fear and yearning. Fantasies of transformation make clear the meaning of the admonition to be careful what we wish lest we be granted it.

Psychology: Through the Eyes of Others—and Ourselves

Skeptical philosophers ask us to imagine possible worlds in which experience is different, more random and unpredictable, than in the world we know. They ask us to visit a possible world in which brains can be transplanted to new bodies, in which we can change our appearance at will, and so on. And they ask how certain we are that *that* world is not *our* world. Our answers reveal not just our beliefs but our hopes and fears.

Psychologists talk about the real world, not just possible alternatives. They remind us that hope and fear are the stuff of everyday experience. For them, the idea of transformation is inescapable. They struggle with a basic dilemma about how to think about human nature. Is it most useful to think of persons as coherent and unified through distinctive characteristics—features that coalesce as our "identity"? Or is identity something of a myth? Are we instead fluid, Protean creatures, always in transformation, remade all the time by our experiences and our own choices? On the first view, fantasies about transformation are brief vacations from our abiding, inescapable selves. On the second view, fantasies of transformation are merely the conscious level of the process of transformation that is our lives.

According to the first view of a coherent and unitary self, our identity has various dimensions. Our physical features are determined by our genes, our DNA. We get just one dip into the genetic pool and are stuck with genetic determinants for life. More controversially, many psychologists argue that characteristic temperaments are equally part of our identity. We are slow or quick to anger, empathetic or self-absorbed, and so on. We typically are consistent over time in our values and goals, likes and dislikes, capacities for language, reasoning, and dispositions to act. Our individual values, reasoning capacities, preferences, distinguish each of us from other selves as significantly as appearance.

This description of a relatively fixed "identity" can prompt conflicting responses. One response is that it is basically true, boringly familiar and pervasive, part of common sense, and everyone's default notion of the self. Another response is to say that it is an ideal of consistency and stability to which we only aspire. But another response is to reject the description—to see it as neither real nor ideal, but rather as myth. Indeed, when science fiction and skeptical philosophy coalesce and seduce us with stories of transformation, they test our common sense reliance on the "fact" that our form is fixed and essentially unchanging. This last response implies that the notions of change and instability are at least as useful in discussing the self as are fixity and stability.

When we ask whether it is more useful to think of persons in terms of either a fixed identity or constant transformation, the question seems pointless in its abstractness. Of course, all of us can be thought of both ways—as having identity and as changing. But the question is useful when we distinguish the point of view of an outsider, a psychologist or a biographer looking at another person (an objective standpoint), from the way we see ourselves (subjectively). Objective coherence is important for biographers; successful biographies show how the parts of the life of Richard Nixon, Charlie Chaplin, or Elizabeth I come together. Sometimes readers see how "the child is father of the man," how talents, influences, and personal limitations determine a life.

Psychologists also look for objective coherence, the patterns that explain our lives. But psychological explanation works only through grasping the subject's self-perception. Psychologists must see how the subject sustains a place in the world, at the identity made up of memories, frustrations, achievements, and goals both satisfied and unsatisfied.

In the rest of this section, I focus on how we see ourselves, not how others see us—and on the place of transformation in such self-understanding. Of course, we have a sense both of our bodies and our ideas, feelings, values, preferences, and goals. These categories are hardly separate. Our goals and values are colored by our sense of the physical impacts we make on the world, and a change in our bodies is likely to have a domino effect in changing our beliefs and behavior.

How well, how stably do we really know our bodies and appearance? We are familiar with pathologies of self-perception. Anorexics and bulimics see themselves as unattractively, unacceptably heavy. But how much *veridical* self-perception is the norm? We all seem to know attractive persons who are dissatisfied with their looks and unattractive ones who consider themselves altogether irresistible. And the fortunes of plastic surgeons suggest that the first group outnumbers the second.

Physical self-awareness is fluid in three ways—with regard to its stability over time (how radically and how often do we change our minds about our appearance?), its normative character (do we like the way we look?), and its veridicality (do we see ourselves as others see us?). The empirical facts that underlie these judgments are elusive. Psychologists can measure when, how, and why people change their minds about their appearance. Whose responses to us do we trust and care about? Observers can document when and why we like or dislike how we look. And they can compare our self-descriptions with what others say about us.

But what is normal and what is pathological? Is it possible to care too much or too little about what others think? Are too many of us under the spell of fads and fashion? Where do facts end and mere opinion begin when we decide that a nose is too large or small or that we are too ethnic in looks or not ethnic enough? We can identify pathologies at the margin, when, for example, thin adults who were fat children have trouble seeing themselves as thin. But once we pass beyond obvious distortion and concede that a self-description is *roughly* true, we run out of ways to measure truth and falsity.

We are also variable in judging whether and how much one should like or dislike one's physical characteristics. We joke about the fact that most persons cringe at the sound of their own recorded voice. We consider such a response so clearly normal that we look askance at those who claim to like their voices. Yet we expect emotionally healthy persons to be content with their appearance. Discontent of the latter kind is thought to mask deeper dislocations of one's sense of self.

We react to the responses of others, and we also construct and create what others see. Most of us most of the time wear clothes, and therefore we must choose what we wear. Even the least self-conscious of us dresses to fit some self-image, some judgment about decorating, enhancing, camouflaging, masking who we are. The decision not to decorate is a decision how to appear, not really different from the most elaborate job of makeup and costuming. And creative decisions about physical appearance go beyond makeup and clothes to the re-shaping of bodies with exercise and plastic surgery.

In this way, we are torn between two models of what we are physically, persons with fixed physiognomies and persons in flux. The first model is that bodies and appearance are fixed, given; we can try at best to decorate, camouflage, and conceal. The alternative is that we are essentially creatures in transformation; we are physically a collaborative work in progress. Dress, exercise, and surgery, far from disguising what we are, allow our real selves to emerge and change. On the first model, the transformative choices we make give the lie to natural truths. They are the stuff of distortion and illusion. On the second model, the distinction between truth and falsity collapses. Literally and figuratively we make ourselves up as we go along.

The same dilemma, the same alternatives haunt our thinking about our beliefs, values, preferences, and goals. For many of us our values and beliefs are the core of our identity, and we seem to have a vital stake in their stability, their integrity. We expect rational persons to have stable values and goals, beliefs that can be tested and refined through argument and consideration of evidence and through consistent actions and choices. We define rational persons as those who are largely unaffected by bias and prejudice and are not malleable in the face of propaganda, or what Orwell aptly called "group-think."

Debates about how rational we are in this sense and about how well we know our own minds echo debates about how well and stably we know our own bodies. Perhaps *everyone's* sense of identity is inherently a work in progress or transition, always at the mercy of new and accidental influences and ideas. We can offer endlessly many stories to support the norm of stable rationality and that of essential changeability. Our working assumptions on these matters say more about our own dispositions and beliefs than about human nature in general.

On a deeper level, these models express hope and fear. We hope that our way of seeing ourselves, planning our actions, judging others, and (in the end) giving meaning to life yield coherent, ordered results and life plans. We fear that experience is in fact something altogether different—less knowable, less ordered, less rational, and more a journey of endless transformation.

Novels, movies, and plays rub our noses in the disorder and irrationality of life, and in the limits of self-knowledge. In literature and life, persons with a well-ordered life plan, engaged in the fixed pursuit of preference satisfaction or pleasure maximization, are likely to be monomaniacs, demagogues, and perpetrators of genocide and conquest. Attila the Hun, Hitler, and Pol Pot all knew what they wanted and tried single-mindedly to achieve their goals. But then so did Michelangelo, Lincoln, and Mother Teresa.

This is not to say that we should want or idealize a disordered or unreflective life, a reactive rather than an active one. But we are more confused about what is true and what is desirable in thinking about human nature than we are likely to admit. Fiction flaunts the irony of these questions; authors, playwrights, and screenwriters offer characters who think they know themselves, who think their lives are ordered and their values are explicit and harmonious—and whose worlds crash and burn. Wisdom is knowing how much we lack wisdom.

While social scientists assume without irony the virtue of being transparent to ourselves, knowing our values, and pursuing them with constancy, literature has always mocked this view. The idea that we live and act within our illusions, and that the world of illusion is precarious, is a literary constant, the common theme of plays from *Oedipus Rex* through *As You Like It* to *Death of a Salesman* and *A Streetcar Named Desire*. The shift from modernism to what is called postmodernism is one of emphasis. Modern novels from *The Great Gatsby* to *Catch-22*, and modern movies from *The Godfather* to *Star Wars*, show how experience plays havoc with everyone's plans and ideals.

In postmodern fiction, the effort to make sense of ourselves and our experiences is self-subverting. The Forrest Gumps of the world, who do not brood about identity or life plans, are by default ironic models of success. Reflecting on who we are and what we stand for has traps, self-delusive lures, that betray us.

The story of identity in our culture is packed with irony. It is really a contest between two stories. One is an ideal of unity and transparency; we know ourselves, have consistent values and goals, and accumulate knowledge. The other stresses self-subversion and change. Because we can fool ourselves about everything we claim to know, we need to take an ironic distance from our values and goals. Who we are and how we see ourselves are nothing but matters in transformation.

The Culture of Transformation

If we hold on to the idea of identity as stable and transparent, we see possible transformations of ourselves only as fictions, as false roles. In this mode we distinguish between a genuine self and its masks. If on the other hand we listen to the nagging voice, we see ourselves as nothing but change and the potential for more change. The distinction between a true self and its masks disappears.

Other persons can make or break our ways of seeing ourselves. They may complement us, play an essential constructive role in building our sense of a coherent, autonomous, and likable self. Or they can be devastatingly threatening and destabilizing. In the 1950s and 1960s, existentialist philosophers disconcerted readers by arguing that we are all endlessly vulnerable to the regard of others. Their point was not the obvious one, that our mood and self-regard may depend on others' responses, but that the presence and attention of others is essentially cannibalistic. Others inevitably take us apart and make us over from their own perspective. To persevere as a person is to resist in a life-and-death struggle.

Before dismissing the existentialist view as hysterical or paranoid, consider one more turn of the theoretical screw. Some psychologists suggest that the battle to defend self-regard against the opinions and responses of others is already lost. In other words, we *are* what others see us to be. We are nothing more than the construction of others, just as they are our constructions in turn. If we are beautiful and think of ourselves that way, it is because others see us as beautiful. If we are smart or generous or mean, it is only by grace of how others see us.

We can question much of this. One may be smart and fail to be recognized as such by one's contemporaries. Nonetheless, reversals of fortune seem to illustrate how much we depend on what others see and do. Victims of brainwashing, systematically deprived of familiar responses, collapse under such assaults and are permanently damaged. Disfigured victims of fire or war, challenged to redefine their relation to strangers and intimates alike, often must create new identities to go with new faces. In less extreme situations, can we really overestimate the effects of recognition on achievement—whether it is recognition of fifth-graders winning chess tournaments, writers winning literary prizes, or movie stars grinning from the covers of *People* and *Entertainment Weekly*? How valid is the belief that, notwithstanding the catastrophe or the honor, one is still the same person, that self-regard should be independent of what others say and do? We use the same term, "recognition," for the process of identifying another person and for applauding that person's achievements, as if the person *is* the sum of what he or she is seen to have done.

If we go back to the hypothesis that human life is a process of constant transformation—of our physical appearance, of our beliefs and values, and of our reflections *about* ourselves—we see how much others are indispensable to self-regard. In a social vacuum, perhaps raised by wolves without any exposure to other persons, you would develop no self-awareness, have no opinions about your appearance, and probably hold only the basic preferences that we attribute to household pets. Any sense of self outside a social setting, outside a social practice with language and conventions, is hardly imaginable.

We owe others our capacity to think about ourselves, and the terms in which we do this thinking, just as much as we owe them our genetic inheritance. The fact that we are born into a specific human society sets up the possibility of self-regard. As part of human society, we gain a language and we learn what roles persons play, what characteristics are praised and blamed, and how social roles are parceled out. We learn, and have to deal with, not just the beliefs widely shared in our society, but the idiosyncratic beliefs of those close to us.

Once we have the tools for thinking about ourselves, life is a struggle with what others think and expect (and with what we think and expect of ourselves). We adopt some ideas and expectations; we reject others. Some parts of this process are conscious; much of it is not.

We have the habit of calling the period of self-definition—of trying on attitudes and roles—adolescence. But perhaps what we call "adolescence" is lifelong; perhaps it is a myth or pathology to achieve a fixed, ossified sense of identity. Presidents and world leaders continue to look wistfully to posterity, the voice of history, or the Gallup poll. Authors are potentially remade by their audiences, professors by their students. Even those who are legendary for resisting their audience—recluses such as J. D. Salinger or judges who go out of their way to make unpopular decisions in the light of justice—may find themselves even more the prisoners and creatures of public opinion than those who establish a truce with it.

It is a truism to say that life is a series of transactions with others in which we manipulate and seek to control, consciously or not, the ways they see us; they, in turn, manipulate *us* through the ways they see us. This applies to physical appearance—clothing, cosmetics, plastic surgery—in which we try to control how others respond and, paradoxically, are controlled by what we regard as their expectations and standards.

We can struggle endlessly with the question of whether we know ourselves better than others know us. Is the "real self" the subject of our own understanding, or do others know us best since they have an image undistorted by rationalization, self-criticism, and self-idealization? Do others see only our masks and not our reality, or are the masks reality?

These questions hardly pose real choices. We can all be indicted for self-delusion, and we all exaggerate our faults or overindulge our virtues. Others, in this sense, appraise us more clearly. But it is just as certain that we harbor thoughts and feelings that are not delusions and that others cannot know. In that sense, we know ourselves best. And our self-regard is a work in progress, a moving target, since we are always checking our judgments by reconsidering how others see us. We struggle to objectivize the subjective—and we fail.

Anthropology and Sociology: Masking Festivals

Skeptical philosophers dissect the continuities of body and mind to show how precariously they make up what we call "identity." Psychologists, in turn, make us reassess ways in which self-experience is stable and ways in which life is continuous transformation. But stories of transformation are not just mind games, not just tools for conceptual scrutiny.

Our myths, religions, and fictions all show a deep fascination with manipulating identity and its implications for evading mortality and disclaiming our social and moral roles. Anthropologists tell us that every culture invents occasions for acting out stories of transformation. Carnival is the generic name for such communal celebrations; Halloween and Mardi Gras are examples.

Carnival is a pretext and context for persons to disguise themselves and become someone else. The French sociologist Roger Caillois notes in *Les Jeux et Les Hommes* that, among primitive civilizations, masks are more commonly found than spears, levers, or bows and arrows. He concludes that no tool, invention, or custom is more universal; the use of masks is recorded in every known civilization.

Historically, masquerade festivals in Europe and the Americas typically mark changes in the seasonal cycles: harvest, the year's end, and the rebirth of nature in spring. Sociologists find ancient origins of carnival in the cult of Osiris in Egypt, the Babylonian origins of the Jewish festival of Purim, Greek celebrations of Dionysius, and in the Roman Kalends, which paid homage to Janus. In the Middle Ages masquerades were often identified with paganism and aggressively suppressed by the Christian church. At the same time, such celebrations as the Feast of Fools, documented in Victor Hugo's *The Hunchback of Notre Dame*, were occasions for the medieval church to mock its own solemnity, to use masquerade and license to parody its own rituals.

In prerevolutionary Europe, the great courts of France and Italy transformed carnival into lavish imperial celebrations, grandly choreographed. At the same time, pagan festivals not unlike pre-Christian ones survived, as they do even now, in isolated corners of Germany, Switzerland, and Austria. In nineteenth-century urban Europe, however, the ascendance of the middle class undermined the rituals and debased many of the social conventions that had defined and individuated earlier societies. The anarchy of masquerade, with its allusions to social turmoil, the licentious, and the irrational, came to play a covert role.

Modern society has tended to suppress and drive into the unconscious the impulses and needs behind festivals of masquerade. But in contemporary America and elsewhere, the resurgent appeal of Halloween remains a measure of our interest and our ambivalence. The myth that Halloween is for children, responsive to their interests alone, gets more threadbare every year.

Let's call all of these various celebrations "festivals of transformation and disguise." They are all distinguished by the fact that one's relations with others are purposefully, if temporarily, reordered. If it is clear that these opportunities serve a deep and nearly universal human need, it is equally clear that their significance is ambiguous and has many facets.

The most obvious and universal aspect is concealment, the paradoxical choice to absent oneself while present. Disguise confers invisibility. What matters is not who one has become, but merely that one is not oneself. The wish and the need to disappear can, in turn, reflect various roles and fantasies.

For example, one may wish to spy on the world, to compare what transpires in one's (apparent) absence with the *normal* goings-on in which one has a part. This may be a kind of inductive checking of whether the events of life follow the same rules when one is not *seen* to be present as observer and monitor. It may be a way of seeing what occurs when one subtracts oneself as a causal element from the world. More practically, it may be a way of checking how others behave, and what they are prepared to say behind one's back.

Concealment enables one to act as well as observe, to be a saboteur as well as a spy. It facilitates crime and dirty tricks. Adequately disguised, the celebrant can spike the punch, pinch flesh, and make off with the silver.

A third and most immediate function of concealment is isolation. Even if one has no wish to spy on others or trick them, one may relish the feeling of being invisible, the assurance that one has put oneself outside familiar commerce with others—the expectations, demands, and acknowledgments that are second nature to us but also clutter our lives. If nothing else, unrecognizability is a kind of vacation.

Disguises not only conceal but are also false appearances, the taking on of a role. Such roles have many forms. In some contexts, many members of a New Orleans krewe, for example, will be masked and dressed identically and therefore indistinguishably. Here the function of disguise is collective and symbolic rather than individual. One puts aside whatever distinguishes oneself and becomes a cog in a shared enterprise. The goal is not simply to be anonymous but to be a living symbol.

On the other hand, maskers at the Venice carnival typically wear individual masks that are formal and stylized. In their lack of expression and their gilded veneer, they have a grandeur and imperviousness that is godlike, disdainful of human imperfection and plainness. Halloween offers a different kind of possibility. Here the emphasis is often on the expressive and the grotesque. Death, deformation, and monstrosity are common themes. Beauty, when pursued at all, is used to mock the exploitation and artificiality of beauty, and common types of costumes include the stripper and the transvestite. Stylization is absent, and horror is never far below the surface.

As often as not, role-playing of this last kind is half-hearted. Grotesque masks are often worn sheepishly, bashfully, almost in a noncommittal way. The mask intimidates the wearer, and the wearer (perhaps) fears the role/mask taking over his life. Disguises that are stylized, purposefully unexpressive, and shared are, in this sense, less daunting and challenging to the wearer. These roles have their prescribed limits and belong to mutually understood rituals. They replace human commerce with a more ordered, externalized structure of relations. The opposite is true for those who indulge the grotesque and the monstrous. Their assumed identity is a challenge to order, a daring and possibly obscene gesture in the face of fate.

What is the deeper meaning and effect of festivals of concealment and disguise? Are they a way for participants to lose themselves or find themselves? Is assuming a role, and being subsumed by it, a way of alienating oneself from the world or becoming intimately involved with it? Does the psychology of masking differ from one culture to another?

The experience of disappearing into a disguise is no doubt a way of recovering and exploring a domain of freedom and irresponsibility. For most people the experience is probably one of ambivalence, the frisson of disorientation along with the shock of unfamiliar possibilities. One can either fall into the role defined by one's false appearance or lapse into the pure passivity of the invisible observer.

The festival participant is like and unlike an actor. Both play roles for limited, well-defined periods. But actors generally are not expected to improvise. Their words typically are scripted. Their audience knows that they are playing such roles, and it sees both identities at once, the identity of the actor along with that of the role. Concealment and disguise are not the main point of the exercise. With festivals of disguise, the opposite is true. There is no script, and there is no audience that monitors the exercise by the conventions of the well-made theater piece. And disguise *is*, for the most part, the raison d'être of the event.

Of course, many of us abstain from festivals of disguise or participate minimally. At Mardi Gras and Halloween, most participants are onlookers. A smear of makeup, a fake mustache, a fragment of costume is often a sufficient, and sufficiently noncommittal, gesture in the direction of assuming a new guise. The element of disguise is repressed and taken as one more pretext for partying. As we have seen, in modern secular cultures Halloween has until recently been seen as primarily a holiday for children.

With philosophy and psychology as effective reminders that identity is a fragile construct, it is easy to see why festivals of disguise might cause trepidation. We are tempted to repress philosophical and psychological truths about what we fear and dislike, relegating them to the domains of theory and therapy. And we are generally successful in doing so. Thus, we forget that it is only by grace of circumstances that our memories and aspirations comfortably coalesce, that we are consistent actors in the lives and expectations of others, and that we take pleasure in an evolving sense of self.

Psychology is, among other things, about the return of the repressed. And our festivals arguably commemorate and celebrate those aspects of life that are most expressive of our hopes and fears. The capacity to change identity, to escape the web of recognition and expectations and to assume a new face and person represents a fantasy that we hardly dare express to ourselves because it puts what we understand about ourselves in question. As Descartes did, it separates the self-knower from what it knows and makes the latter contingent. The strangeness of festivals of disguise is that they institutionalize and sanctify that fantasy.

Acting

The relationship between acting and identity is complex and problematic. Audiences, even if they are made up of young children, can usually distinguish the actor from her roles. The role itself is typically not the creation of the actor but of the playwright; the actor is the medium through which the playwright speaks to the audience. The actor, more often than not, shares his or her appearance with the character. And the actor plays the character only for a clearly marked and limited time in a clearly delineated, artificial space. This is as true of movie and television actors as it is of those onstage.

And yet there is a sense in which the actor becomes the character or in which the audience is led (fooled? tricked?) into taking the actor as his character. Soap opera fans write letters of advice and condolence when characters suffer adversity; actors who play villains are hissed on the street. This confusion taps something essential in acting. Reality and illusion must coexist or the performance is stillborn. The performance is, paradoxically, a sleight of hand in which the audience is *in on the illusion*. How can this be so, and how have we come to revere such performances as our most public and culturally important kind of diversion? How do actors achieve their tricks, and why do they play important roles in so many lives, so many fantasies?

From the standpoint of identity, actors seem to have their cake while eating it. While remaining themselves, they get to try out other personae. They can experience being jealous, terminally ill, or endangered without reaping the dire consequences of these predicaments. Thus, they inhabit more than one personality at a time.

But while many of us envy the looks or finances of the most successful actors, we may not at the same time envy their everyday lives. Putting aside the obvious drawbacks, such as compromised privacy, we are likely to see their choice of career as problematic and their special gift for it as a mixed blessing. Historically, actors were seen as persons of dubious virtue and questionable trust. The reasons for this, if no longer held, are at least understandable.

If stability of identity is fragile and hard-won, if it is at the mercy of the attitudes and responses of others, then the deliberate taking on of alien identities is a remarkably risky and puzzling way to spend one's life. First of all, it carries the flavor of deceit, of fooling others about one's feelings, opinions, and character. (If you can fool me while you're onstage, you can fool me anytime and are not to be trusted.) Secondly, it seems to put the actor in jeopardy of not knowing his or her true feelings, true self. How much difference is there between simulating a feeling or characteristic on film or stage and making the feeling your own, becoming the character you portray? Actors, in so-called "real life," may slip into the personae of their roles. Thirdly, it transforms a process that is largely unconscious and spontaneous, the sum of one's mutually recognitive transactions with others, into a process that is necessarily deliberate and planned. How easy is it for actors to slip back into unscripted and authentic responses to others (and what does the notion of authenticity come to mean)? And finally, it creates a dissonance with an audience that expects the actor to embody his role, expects Sylvester Stallone to *be* Rocky or Rambo and Carroll O'Connor to be Archie Bunker.

There are more conundrums about the motivation of actors. Do they experience themselves as empty vessels to be filled by their roles? Do they, on the other hand, see themselves as fully formed persons, but ones who try to disclaim, disown their familiar selves? Or are both of these suggestions just myths? Do actors come to realize and know themselves better through acting, so that the process is largely therapeutic? Or, as suggested above, is acting a constant threat because it seems to diffuse and confuse a sense of personal consistency and integrity?

No doubt it is possible to cite evidence for all these possibilities. Just as they come in all shapes and sizes, actors come in infinitely many psychological flavors—some with an unusually fragile sense of their identity, others with a robust ego; some who become actors to camouflage shyness by assuming other selves, others who take on roles in a spirit of extroversion and of testing their own capacities; some disposed to blend their personalities with their characters, others able to turn acting on and off at will. What is interesting for our purposes is not what dispositions actors bring to the job but the job itself. The job is inherently that of being a chameleon.

Scholars of the theory of acting dispute whether acting comes essentially from inside or outside. The distinction is relevant both in training actors and in their practice as professionals. Should they be taught, as so-called "method" actors claim, to empathize with their characters, to live their characters' lives by reconstructing a history for them and a special way of being oriented to the world? Does acting, in other words, grow out of feeling what one's character would feel? Or, on the other hand, is it constructed from outside, with emphasis not on the interior life of the actor, but on the interpersonal transaction with an audience, on the ability to convey an illusion of life and feeling through tone and gesture regardless of what the actor may feel?

The first way of thinking is said to represent American attitudes toward acting, the latter British ones. Thus, the caricature of method actors is that they are wracked with problems of identity, that they suffer all the disabilities of their characters *along with* confusions of personal identity. The caricature of British actors is that they are illusionists, magicians who use appearance and intonation as sleight of hand.

In practice, many actors will admit that both caricatures are just that, caricatures. Only a pathologically disturbed actor will systematically mistake personal feelings for those of the character or be confused for long about his or her own identity. And hardly any actor will insist that empathy plays no part in acting.

The distinctiveness of acting lies not in these caricatures but in the fact that acting inevitably touches on all the unsettling aspects of identity and transformation explored in this chapter. It approximates and even mimics the skeptic's project whereby a new set of feelings and attitudes (that of the character) is seen to inhabit a familiar body (that of the actor). For the actor who alters his appearance, the experience is the inverse skeptical possibility, whereby the actor's own feelings, memories, and continuity of experience appear to the audience in a new body. Thus, the actor is the exemplary manipulator and tester of our psychological assumptions about the self and others. His assumed identity is a construct of how others perceive him. The stability of his self-identity and its independence of the responses of others are put to the test in every instance of acting.

Even if the question of whether acting occurs "essentially" inside or outside the actor is a false question, the alternatives identify two extremes of acting. In the first case, the actor does nothing to change appearance but effects the role

The Culture of Transformation

entirely through voice and movement. The actor's *normal* appearance is always present, and the audience sees double, the actor and the role. In the second case, the actor is wholly disguised, buried by makeup and costuming. The role is all the audience sees. Again, for many actors, most experiences lie between these extremes, as they try to use some physical alteration in makeup and costume to keynote the role and mark off its boundaries. But the second of the two possibilities raises acutely the themes of this book. In that case, the actor's identity is wholly, if temporarily, in limbo; recognition by others is wholly a response to what he creates rather than who he is. He has, in a sense, disappeared from the interpersonal world and been superseded.

Chapter 3

The
Art of
Transformation

It is only shallow people who do not judge by appearances.

Man is least himself when he talks in his own person.
Give him a mask and he will tell the truth.

OSCAR WILDE, *Aphorisms*

Transformation as Craft

What is the art of transformation? Is there something pretentious and off-putting in placing the work of makeup artists among the fine arts?

Roughly defined, arts seem to involve creative activities that enrich life while being inessential to it, that are not instrumental but are worth doing for their own sake. But trying to define the arts is a bit like trying to grab hold of a sphere of mercury. The arts elude definition. Even philosophers, whose business is conceptual analysis, have never had an easy time with the arts. Aesthetics has always been the black sheep in the philosophical flock. While philosophers have tried, for greater or less success, to build a life's work and argue across the centuries about knowledge, goodness, or truth, they have usually stumbled embarrassingly when they have discussed the beautiful (or for that matter, the grotesque).

Why are the arts something of a mystery? We all feel the appeal of stories, but do we know why stories move and fascinate us? Do we understand the appeal of music, of visual art? When any of these arts *work*, they do so by triggering emotions, not just simple emotions like anger and love but complex and varied emotions for which we hardly have names. If we are dumbstruck in the face of explaining art, it is largely because we are daunted by the job of understanding and explaining our emotions.

The link between art and emotion is only one of the challenges in understanding art. A related challenge is that the experience of art is idiosyncratic. A picture or song or movie taps into a private history of associations, an internal history unique to each of us. When we try to explain or criticize the experience, we must tap those common elements that we think we share with others. But this hardly does justice to the effect of the work of art on any particular individual.

These two aspects—the link of art and emotion, the idiosyncratic experience of art—show how much of an understatement is the claim that a picture is worth a thousand words. An infinity of words will not do either. Read a reporter's or critic's account of a concert you haven't heard, a picture you haven't seen. If you are unfamiliar with the artist's or the composer's style, the account falls maddeningly short of communicating the experience.

Language fails art not only because the experience of art is emotional and personal. Even if there are shared ways in which Michelangelo, Mozart, Keats, Kandinsky, and the Beatles speak to their audience, we become largely inarticulate when we try to translate that appeal into words. This does not mean that art criticism, music criticism, and their kin lack any purpose, only that they are poor adjuncts to direct experience.

This book argues that the appeal and fascination of an uncelebrated kind of art, living faces created by makeup artists, has this kind of resonance. Chapter 2 explored the cognitive and cultural role of the twin ideas of identity and transformation. Our stories, our rituals, our fantasies return again and again to the impossibility and the lure of transformation, with its implications for mortality, responsibility, and self-regard. But an explanation of an art is peripheral to the art itself. If the art fails to excite us, the explanation is beside the point. If the art does engage us, then the explanation merely complements the emotion, the appeal, and the bemusement.

The accomplishments of transformational makeup artists, as we saw in Chapter 1, differ from most visual art in four ways. They are a kind of trompe l'oeil so that they work when we are fooled into thinking the artifact is natural.

They are alive, in that the object is a living, moving face. They are ephemeral, in that (like performance art) they are of short duration, and they begin to deteriorate soon after they are finished. And finally, our full appreciation of them as art is paradoxical, in the sense that (the trompe l'oeil aspect notwithstanding) we can only appreciate them if we can *see through* them, if we experience them as natural while understanding them as artifacts.

The standard view of the art of makeup is that it is functional and peripheral. For the movie audience, it is one of the arsenal of special effects that liberate filmmakers from the constraints of reality and that paradoxically allow them to mimic kinds of reality that cannot occur on the soundstage. Only devout fans of science fiction or gore are likely to know how skin can melt away to reveal the metal substructure of a robot, or how arms and heads are raggedly lobbed off.

For actors, special effects makeup is likely to be peripheral to their main work. Rarely do parts mandate radical transformation, and most actors will never have to deal with latex prosthetics in their entire careers. A few may be the Lon Chaneys of their generation and thrive on chameleonhood. A few others may stumble into popular success as alien leads in a successful science fiction television series, trapped into being Quark or Worf *(Star Trek)* or G'Kar *(Babylon 5)* for much of a decade. But they are the exceptions, and their hours undercover are hardly envied by their peers.

Even makeup artists appreciate that their contribution to movies, ads, or television shows are typically one cog in the success of the whole enterprise, often unnoticed and unremarked. Critics tend to dismiss their work as a distraction, lamenting that actors have to do their work under "forty pounds of rubber" or in "Halloween masks." But even if makeup artists see themselves more as technicians than artists, they have an unarticulated sense of the artistic motives that fuel them, motives that have hardly ever been taken seriously by critics.

The next two sections identify what these makeup artists do and who they are. They examine the roles of the two other players in these artistic events, the actor, who is both artist's canvas and performer, and the audience, which is both collaborator in and dispeller of illusion.

How to Make a Face

Artistry always comes in the *how* rather than the *what*. The difference between a hack drummer and a pro, a hack writer and a pro is not in what they do (both beat drums, both process words) but in how they do it. And for most arts, we hardly need to be told the simple rudiments of what writers, violinists, painters, costumers, and playwrights do.

But with makeup artists, as perhaps with architects and graphic artists, the most basic steps of the job are not common knowledge. The basic technique is simple and has hardly changed in forty years. The art of prosthetic transformation involves sheathing the face, and sometimes the body, in pieces of simulated skin usually made of foam latex (prosthetic appliances), and then making the whole appear to be a natural face or a natural body. The appliances, attached to the face at every point, are designed to move with facial muscles, to reflect expression perfectly. Nearly weightless, they are designed to be minimal encumbrances to the wearer.

That, at least, is the aspiration. The earliest prosthetic appliances, popular in the 1940s and 1950s, were one-piece masks. Their relative immobility prompted two developments. The first stressed the importance of thinness. The mantra "thinner is better" is less controversial with regard to prosthetics than personal weight management. But thin appliances are delicate, hard to produce, and hard to apply. The second innovation, generally attributed to Dick Smith, the single greatest innovator and teacher in the field, is the use of multiple overlapping partial appliances. Smith set a new standard and achieved uncanny results in such movies as *Little Big Man* and *Amadeus* by using such appliances.

Today, general practice varies with the artist and the job. Some artists still use continuous pieces (masks) that cover much of the face with startling success. Others swear by the now-common practice of using separate, thin, overlapping pieces for forehead, nose, cheekbones, undereye bags, jowls, and so on. (In *The Nutty Professor*, Rick Baker used different techniques for the different Eddie Murphy personae. The more delicately featured characters, Mother Klump for example, involved overlapping appliances, while the coarser ones, such as Sherman Klump's brother, used prosthetic masks.)

Foam latex appliances fall short in two other troubling ways. Even at its thinnest, the material rarely moves—folds, creases, stretches—in quite the way flesh does. The quest for materials—new formulas of latex, new alternatives to latex—remains this industry's equivalent of the Holy Grail. Several artists, most enthusiastically Gordon Smith and Greg Cannom, use and commend new silicone rubber materials, while others (for example, Matthew Mungle in *Ghosts of Mississippi* and the crew at Steve Johnson's XFX Inc.) have revived interest in gelatin-based materials. Both materials have their drawbacks. Silicone materials are said to be hard to attach and process; gelatin deteriorates in ways that latex does not. In any case, defectors from the foam latex camp are in the minority, although many dabble in the chemistry of the process and devise their own formulas.

The other defect is that foam latex does not reflect light as flesh does. Skin is translucent, latex opaque. Appliances tend to reflect light with a rubbery sheen or dullness. Alongside the cottage industry of reconfiguring the chemical structure of foam latex is a parallel industry of devising special paints and colors that give latex the appearance of skin. Airbrushing is a widely used and effective painting technique.

How do appliances come into being? Although so-called generic appliances can sometimes be used with impressive success, appliances typically are made for particular actors and are not reusable. The process begins with the need for a cast of the actor's face or head. Alginate, applied like a thick mudpack over the actor's face and head, dries in about fifteen minutes, yielding a negative impression in perfect detail. Skin texture, pores, the finest lines and wrinkles are all fully marked in the alginate if it is applied correctly. A positive cast, a life mask or bust of the actor, is produced from the alginate negative. The cast is sturdy, reusable, and as finely detailed as possible. The new face is then sculpted over the life cast, typically in clay or a similar modeling material.

The fact that the new face is sculpted over the old points up two obvious limitations of the transformation process. The process is always one of addition rather than subtraction. When the new character's face is in fact fleshier, fuller, rounder than the actor's own, the process can be straightforward. But when the new face must be spare flesh stretched over bone, when the new face has the sunken cheeks and eroded flesh of age, the sculptor must perform the magic of making addition look like subtraction.

A second obvious limitation is that the new face will have the essential bone structure of the old. The makeup artist cannot make widely spaced eyes together or make a jutting chin into a receding one. Here again there is often a need for illusionary magic, and some of the masterworks of makeup convince us that we can trace a new skeleton under the flesh.

Once the clay is worked into a finished sculpture, this image serves as the positive from which a negative cast is created. The space between two plaster casts, this new negative and the positive cast of the actor's face, will conform exactly to the shape of the three-dimensional prosthetic appliance. After the foam latex is mixed in a viscous liquid form, it is injected between the two casts. The sandwich, with the latex mix filling the space between the casts, is baked to cure the latex, turning it into foam rubber appliances. The underside of the appliance fits the actor's face, and the outside perfectly renders the new features.

Prosthetic appliances may be partially painted before they are glued to the actor's face. Typically, they are painted after they are applied. The former saves the actor's time; it is an option when appliances cover the face more or less completely. Most artists use surgical adhesives which create an effective bond for a long day of filming, and special solvents are needed to restore the actor's natural face. Thus, the dramatic gesture of ripping off the mask to reveal the actor beneath is hardly to be recommended, since much of the actor's flesh would come off as well.

Painting and blending the appliances come after the artist creates a perfectly seamless surface. Liquid latex or similar substances are used to make the edges of appliances, where they meet flesh and where they meet other appliances, altogether invisible. The edges themselves are tissue-thin.

Finally, the process of painting is more complex and more idiosyncratic for each artist than one would guess. Because it involves the near impossibility of making opaque appliances look translucent, it requires layering color and shadows, many layers and many colors. The artist anticipates the kind of light in which faces will be seen and the ways in which appliances will reflect such light. No appliance and no paint job is likely to look realistic in all lights and all circumstances.

Like sculptors and architects, prosthetic makeup artists are engineers and applied scientists. They use information from chemistry, engineering, materials technology, and other fields to work their effects. Some makeup artists use computers as an adjunct to sculpting, moving planes of the face and redesigning features on the screen before molding clay. Some even predict that computers may allow makeup artists to bypass the messy process of alginate casting, that they may soon be able to do a laser scanning of an actor's face and use the information to duplicate the face in a hard, three-dimensional medium.

But, as in other arts, it is inconceivable that makeup artists will ever become pure technicians or that technological processes will make their art obsolete. Technology cannot displace the artists' decisions about just how the burdens of life will turn a young face old, or how a benign alien that has lived for millenia will look, or how an actor who looks nothing like Jack Kennedy can be made to convince us he *is* the ex-president. The arts of designing, sculpting, applying, and painting appliances will be obsolete only when actors are obsolete because they too have been replaced by sophisticated animation, only when Bart Simpson routinely puts Brad Pitt out of work.

Who the Facemakers Are

There are no university majors, few graduate programs, and almost no trade schools for makeup artists. To the extent that such limited courses or programs do exist, they have produced few of the best-known character makeup artists. One reason is that courses are offered to college-age and older students. By the time they were approaching their twenties, many top makeup artists had already been proficient for half a decade.

More than any other film-related craft, makeup artistry is a calling that makes itself evident early. Actors, screenwriters, directors, scenic designers often segue into their specialty as adults after trying out several professions. By contrast, virtually all of the most successful makeup artists knew by the time they entered their teens that, more than anything, they wanted to create faces and invent persons. If the spark often came from horror movies, from *Frankenstein* to *The Exorcist*, most say they understood early that the finer crafts of aging and subtle character creation would be their best challenges. And most affirm that they spent their high school years often alone in garages and at kitchen ovens, sculpting and curing rubber.

The makeup artist's mix of skills and learning, from sculpting and painting to the chemistry of materials and the health effects of adhesives and paints, and even to the psychology of preventing claustrophobic breakdowns by actors buried in alginate, is wide and diverse. For the most part, they are self-taught. Or, rather, their preparation combines solitary investigation, trial-and-error experimentation, and apprenticeship. The last of these stages is the most distinctive.

The maturation of a modern makeup artist mimics the career of a medieval artisan, who served an apprenticeship in one or another guild, participating increasingly in the work of the master craftsman and refining his art communally. Virtually all of these makeup artists, both those who went on to set up their own studios and those who prefer to work alone, spent time in the studio of an established major artist. Many have been journeyman artists, moving through several studios. And, because studios are continuously taking on artists for particular projects, joining with other studios for other projects, or losing artists who go off on their own, almost everyone has worked with everyone else at one time or another.

Although it is impossible to do justice to networks of influence, to associations and rivalries, it is possible to offer a few generalizations. The community of character makeup artists remains small. If it is roughly as old as the film industry itself, the modern innovations in materials and techniques that are still state of the art have their roots in the 1950s and 1960s in the work of such masters as Dick Smith *(The Exorcist, Little Big Man, Amadeus)* and John Chambers *(The List of Adrian Messenger, Planet of the Apes)*. Indeed, Dick Smith remains a seminal teacher through a newsletter and courses on technique and technology. In his generosity he seems to have had a crucial influence on every important artist of recent generations.

This book looks at the work of the contemporary generation of artists, for the most part in their forties or younger. Some maintain large, multipurpose studios with many artists and technicians; others prefer to work by themselves. Most are in southern California, corralled within eight or ten miles of each other in "the Valley" (the San Fernando Valley). Others (for example, Carl Fullerton,

John Caglione Jr., Norman Bryn) are incorrigibly East Coasters/New Yorkers. Still others—Tom Savini in Pittsburgh, Gordon Smith in Toronto, Crist Ballas in St. Paul—keep a safe distance from turmoil and choose to work in the middle of the continent. And interesting work is done by makeup studios in England, Sweden, and elsewhere. Larger makeup studios in the United States are, of course, exclusively near Los Angeles where the major movie and television production companies provide the elephant's share of work.

Contrasts and comparisons are endless. Each studio, and each individual, markets a distinctive range of skills. For the full-line studios that take on so-called "creature effects" for such break-the-bank blockbusters as *Starship Troopers* and *Men in Black*, prosthetic makeup effects are one part of a smorgasbord of effects and illusions that include animatronics and computer simulation. Rick Baker's Cinovation Studios is perhaps the best-known example of a studio that offers a full range of creature-creating services (a kind of versatility extravagantly displayed in *Men in Black*) and maintains preeminence in prosthetic transformational art *(The Nutty Professor)*. Stan Winston Studios and Greg Cannom's Cannom Creations are also full-service studios that do more than prosthetic transformation. Among newer studios, Todd Masters' company, MastersFX, has growing visibility and influence as it maintains a similar balance between a stream of disarmingly convincing traditional prosthetic transformations and a full range of other products. Other large studios, among them ADI (Alec Gillis and Tom Woodruff Jr.) and KNB (Greg Nicotero and Howard Berger), are best known for animatronic and horror effects but have regularly perpetrated subtle prosthetics with success.

Science fiction on television has been a perilous endeavor, even more so for production companies that have seen costly projects self-destruct than for fictional time-and-space travelers themselves. *Babylon 5* was a succès d'estime with a select audience (and dramatically so with worldwide fans) while the various *Star Trek* series have come to define sci-fi television for many viewers. John Vulich's Optic Nerve Studios fashioned some of the most convincing and seductive aliens of all time for *Babylon 5*. Mike Westmore, the current mainstay of a family that defined Hollywood makeup expertise for decades, has in recent years operated in-house at Paramount, supervising the makeup needs of many *Star Trek* projects. Both Vulich and Westmore specialize in prosthetic appliances. Like Vulich's Optic Nerve, Steve Johnson's XFX Inc. has a record of eclectic success in science fiction and horror, with a particular notoriety in evoking the demonic effectively enough, one assumes, to stir the envy of real demons.

The market for makeup transformations, as we saw in Chapter 1, is skewed. Megabudget science fiction and action films offer the most frequent and lucrative employment for makeup artists, needs that are often satisfied by the larger studios with the most varied bags of tricks. Although makeup artists often say that subtle character transformations—young to old, historical figures—are their most satisfying challenges, such opportunities are comparatively rare. Such projects often go to those individual artists who work alone or run small studios and have carved their own special niche. Kevin Haney, Carl Fullerton, Matthew Mungle, and Gordon Smith have all been responsible for various kinds of joltingly convincing transformations, too often for uncelebrated and barely noticed movies, commercials, and television shows. Increasingly they work in conjunction with larger houses on projects that require a range of services and skills.

No less than screenwriters and actors, makeup artists can have feast-or-famine roller-coaster careers, dependent on the momentum of their latest success and on the kindness of friends. Unlike screenwriters and actors, their work involves a large capital investment in equipment and space. Maintaining a steady and growing practice is a high-wire act, more so for the high-rent, high-investment, large studio than for the individual who crafts rubber in his garage. And the most consistent careers have not always been the most celebrated and visible; celebrity can be an invitation to overexposure and overinvestment. The steadiest careers, as in most fields, have belonged to the artists' artists, often solitaries, who are sought by their peers as a last, best resort for the art of the impossible.

For various reasons, prosthetic transformation is a young artist's art. We saw that inspiration comes early, and most of these artists are self-taught and well apprenticed by the time they are out of their teens. Moreover, the current and continuing demand for extravagant science fiction (movies and television), bloody action, and sickeningly realistic gore is only as old as *Star Wars*, *The Exorcist*, and *The Godfather*. If the techniques are older, the industry spawned by these genre-building movies is not. In that sense, the 1980s and 1990s have been a Golden Age for effects innovators of all stripes. New fields, wedding new and old technologies, have developed and have quickly stabilized with mature cohorts of youngish, recognized, and competing artists.

The world of transformational makeup artists is oddly homogeneous. Age is just one shared factor, with the most interesting and prolific artists mostly clustered between their late twenties and late forties. Relatively few women and minority artists seem drawn to transformational makeup, in sharp contrast to the related field of cosmetic or beautification makeup. (These traditional jobs of makeup, both in enhancing actors' looks and in preparing them to look "natural" under the bright lights of soundstages, have always been shared by men and women.) Largely self-taught and rarely college-educated, the makeup artists I came to know in preparing this book are articulate, well read, and remarkably thoughtful. They are unpretentious both in manner and appearance. Unlike cosmetic artists, who often and appropriately see themselves as walking advertisements for their craft, transformational makeup artists may look indistinguishable from other artists, sculptors, or for that matter individual contractors in plumbing or construction. And, in person, they rarely embody the attitudes and postures that outsiders cherish in their clichés about Hollywood.

Actors as Canvases

Actors are usually not comfortable having their features obliterated with makeup. But they run the gamut. Some prefer to act without makeup. This conviction fits a certain theory of acting, the idea that true acting comes from "inside" and that cosmetics and costumes are crutches rightly disdained. For others, makeup and costumes are essential. A scar, a birthmark, or a gaudy shirt is the external hook that distinguishes the actor from his part, the physical seed out of which the character grows. But only rarely do actors carry this to its logical extreme, finding inspiration and liberation in total concealment, total transformation.

In Chapter 2 we looked at the psychological identification of actors with their roles. Views ranged from "method acting," whereby acting means nurturing and embodying what the character feels, to the contrasting idea that actors use technique, tricks of voice and gesture, to prompt an emotional response from the audience. This debate has little to do with attitudes toward makeup. The method actor may or may not use physical transformation as part of his or her project of embodying a character, and an actor who sees the part externally may or may not include major physical changes as part of an armory of conjuring tricks.

Prosthetic makeup presents an obvious practical challenge. Even the thinnest and lightest appliance inhibits the actor's expressions. Each actor must relearn to act through rubber, and success depends on both the actor and the makeup. Some actors find any rubber fatally distracting and inhibiting. And some maladroit makeups will defeat all attempts at expression and subtlety of characterization.

The tradition of acting through immobile masks is of course as old as theater itself. The training of contemporary actors typically includes maskwork as a way to focus on the theatrical effects of voice and gesture. Specialized forms of acting have always built on the challenge of subtraction; mime subtracts the interpretive tool of voice, and masks subtract the tool of facial expression.

But in these respects prosthetic makeup is not at all to be confused with masks. Masks inherently limit flexibility of natural expression and are designed to do so; prosthetic makeup does so only to the extent that it is badly done, only as a drawback and limitation. The actor's job is not, as with masks, to devise a specialized and stylized technique of communication but to tame the rubber into as natural a physical rendering as possible.

More often than not, critics are left high and dry by actors in makeup, not knowing how much to credit the performer and how much to credit the makeup. Confronting Eddie Murphy's utterly convincing incarnation of Klumps of various ages and genders in *The Nutty Professor*, along with Rick Baker's state-of-the-art prosthetic transformations, critics grumpily expressed a nostalgic preference for the pure mimicry of his *Saturday Night Live* routines. Sourly, they questioned the necessity of "forcing" James Woods to act through age prosthetics in *Ghosts of Mississippi*.

Even when the challenge of acting through rubber is met and the critics are seduced, prosthetic transformation presents a special case of acting. Paradoxically, the actor is in one sense passive, the makeup artist's canvas. In another sense, he has a special relationship to the makeup artist, because the artist's vision is added to that of the scriptwriter, the director, and others in shaping the performance. The makeup artist, along with others, determines the character's history, attitudes, and opportunities through the invented face.

This duality—as canvas and as animator of the sculptor's vision—is both a threat and an opportunity for the actor. The threat is that one parameter of the actor's ability to monitor the distinction between himself and his roles disappears. In most roles most of the time, the actor need only look in the mirror to find a reminder of his real identity. As the canvas for a radical makeup transformation, the actor loses this parameter. Alan Gray, posing for Steve Johnson's demonstration of a demonic makeup, was admonished by his wife, "I can't find you in there."

The process of being subsumed by the makeup can often take three or four hours. Typically, actors arrive at the soundstage hours before anyone else except the artists charged with applying the prosthetics. By the time the rest of the cast arrives and shooting begins, they will have witnessed their own metamorphosis into unrecognizability. And they will not undergo the one-hour-or-more process of recovering their own persona until everyone else has gone home. Often, over the course of several days or weeks of production, the other actors will not know them except as their characters. When they finally meet other actors with whom they have shared endless hours of work and casual conversation, and do so in their own identity, they are strangers.

Whether this kind of experience is a threat or an opportunity for an actor (and obviously it is both), it is certainly distinctive. It is an everyday instance of the myth of invisibility, of the fantasy of passing through life unrecognized. The actor may be unmoored by it. Or he may be invigorated by it as the purest opportunity for acting, a chance to face an audience that has no expectations based on who he really is. The audience is blind not only to his name, private life, and other roles. It may not even have a clue as to his age or real appearance.

There may be as many ways of understanding acting as there are actors. Radical prosthetic transformation gives the actor a resource he does not normally have, but at the same time it threatens to inhibit his use of other resources. It gives him one more master and one more set of ideas to serve and express, since he embodies the ideas of the makeup artist. And it gives him an unconventional, possibly anarchic, relationship to his audience.

The Audience: On Being Fooled

The new technology of special effects is designed to make the work of the audience easier. Until the last twenty years, the demands of moviemaking created a kind of cognitive dissonance. Our eyes saw, and our minds confirmed, that the creature in the black lagoon could be nothing but a man in a crude rubber suit and that the spaceship was a toy made of tin foil precariously positioned against a black velvet screen. We had to struggle to suspend disbelief. The new technology makes the struggle easy; what we see is utterly convincing.

Transformational makeup is in a perilous situation as one of the new special effects. It carries over a technology that is much older, much more low tech, than that which allows us to show space battles or the destruction of Washington, D.C. And yet it must satisfy the same level of expectation. It must have the same gloss.

The audience, even when it knows it is being fooled, wants the eye to be fooled completely, to be taken in by the perfect image, the perfect deception. When it comes to characters in transformational makeup, the deception is of course twofold. It includes both the traditional investment of belief that the actor is the character portrayed, and the additional belief that the actor really looks like that character.

But there's a difference between these two kinds of deception. No one (or almost no one) believes that Brad Pitt, Julia Roberts, or Robert DeNiro really *is* the character portrayed, any more than anyone believes (however much some may wish it) that Washington has really been reduced to rubble. But the art of the makeup artist sometimes crosses the line, or at least is designed to do so and aspires to do so. When it really succeeds, we may be convinced, may have no doubt, that the actor appears as he or she does.

Even this distinction does not capture what is special about the effects of the makeup artist's illusion. The best job of aging may convince us that the actor is profoundly old and the best incarnations of Nixon may excite all our Nixon-based passions, but no makeup artist will leave us without misgivings about whether the actors playing aliens really lack noses and ears. And the completely unquestioned illusion *can* occur elsewhere. We may have no reason to question that the lovers are embracing in the middle of traffic in Times Square even when a complex blue screen and matte layering of images produce the illusion.

What seduces and unsettles us uniquely with makeup illusions is the sense of a personal encounter, the subliminal assurance that we could spontaneously meet and interact with these invented beings as persons, just as we have intercourse with natural persons in unscripted, unfilmed life. And in a sense, we almost can. The ideal to which the makeup artist aspires is the transformation that can succeed in the circumstances of life, a character that can step out of the frame, off the screen, and proceed with a life of its own.

In other words, the makeup illusion goes beyond what is necessary to make the movie, the TV series, the advertisement work. It works in a way that can be called *metaphysical*. The actor playing a role will, we know, stop playing it when the camera stops rolling. The volcano that engulfs Los Angeles does so, however convincingly, only for the camera. Even the Batmobile exists as a nine-inch plastic model. Our eyes, which are perfectly taken in, and our minds, which are also in on the deception, are perfectly synchronized and metaphysically at peace.

But, if I am right, what disturbs us about the makeup illusion (and what is the explicit goal of the makeup process) is the creation of an autonomous physical being that can assume a distinct physical and natural presence. It can intrude in our world, reveal a life history, unleash an arsenal of its own expressions and responses, just as real persons with their expressive repertoires and genetically determined physiognomies can do. The movie is the occasion of the illusion, but it hardly contains it, hardly exhausts it.

For these reasons, as we have already seen, the work of makeup artists has special significance. If we think of them usurping the godlike role of creating artificial beings that mimic physically and metaphysically the work of nature and genetic history, we also think of them as guardians at the threshold of closely guarded cultural fantasies about identity and transformation.

This account of the audience's transaction with makeup artists makes broad assumptions. Perhaps most audiences and most makeup artists never ask themselves about the implications of what they experience and create. Perhaps I am plainly wrong about what their responses would be. The purpose of my inquiry is not to nail down the characteristics of an art form, but to stir interest and suggest possibilities.

Arts need to create their audiences. As a peripheral craft for movie and television effects, the art of transformational makeup has hardly had much of a distinctive audience. That audience, such as it is, is fragmentary, and those who are sophisticated either as artists themselves or aficionados of the art are typically self-labeled eccentrics. The job of recognizing and legitimating an audience for this art is twofold. It must uncover a sense of the uncanny, a sense, in the creations of makeup artists, of something evocative, something that draws our attention and leaves us with feelings that elude easy explanation. It must also situate the activity, as much as possible, within a web of evolving self-understanding.

Part two of this book, as it explores the different projects of makeup artists and illustrates their successes, tries to identify the point at which the metaphysical frontier is crossed and our eyes tell us that a new individual with a claim to a life of its own exists.

Part II

The Practice of
Transformation

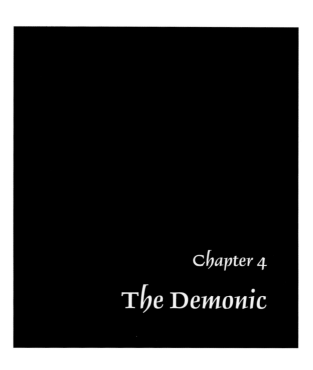

Chapter 4

The Demonic

There is nothing that fear or hope does not make men believe.

VAUVENARGUES

The basis of optimism is sheer terror.

OSCAR WILDE

On Horror

Your first thought about makeup is probably about the imperative of making persons look good. Only as an afterthought is it evident that some makeup artists do the opposite, make persons look bad (in both senses, ugly and evil). The work of makeup artists, when not a matter of enhancement, is generally associated with horror effects. Frankenstein, Dracula, and the Wolfman are, one assumes, what transformational makeup in the movies is all about, the archetypes.

One aim of this book is to show how much of a misconception this is. The creation of new faces and the transformation of the actors wearing them can

serve many purposes. In fantasy we may want to become many things, to have limitless choices among possible personae—and becoming repulsive may be low on that list. Movies may require actors to be transformed into aliens, historical figures, or mutants, or they may be about the use of disguise itself. In fact, many makeup artists lament the fact that their talents are used often for so-called "gore effects" and rarely for jobs of possibly greater subtlety and variety. Some decline to work on horror.

And yet horror is not to be written off so fast. The most popular Halloween masks are designed to scare. For sixty years horror films have been a robust genre. These facts are, it seems, easily explained. We like to scare and be scared, to tell (and act out) stories that unsettle others, and to be disturbed ourselves, reminded of our vulnerability and mortality.

Why should that be? Terrifying others affirms one's power and control; when one does so by donning a horrific mask, power can be acted out with relative safety for terrifier and terrified alike, and all are playacting. *Being* terrified by gore movies and horror stories seems a way of confronting the worst that can happen and surviving it. Bodies and body parts may litter the screen, but we walk out of the theater more or less intact. On an even simpler level, vicarious terror allows us one kind of vacation from the predictable routine of much that we do and a respite from emotional entanglements. The predicaments in horror are elemental, and the appropriate reaction is visceral.

When makeup artists connive to terrify us, they make actors look "bad." But the term is ambiguous. The job is not just to bring revulsion at ugliness. The appearance of ghouls has to reflect a malign nature. The creations must not merely be bad-looking; their looks must be clear evidence of single-mindedly bad intent.

The inescapable idea here may be ideologically troubling and "politically incorrect," biased against those who are ill-favored in appearance. We associate beauty with moral goodness and ugliness with evil. Some great works of literature play variations on that association, suggesting that it is a lure and a mistake. *The Hunchback of Notre Dame* shows that a good soul can inhabit a repulsive body, while *The Picture of Dorian Gray* connects physical seductiveness to evil. But these are the exceptions. Countless stories, movies, and television shows reinforce the nearly universal notion that heroic persons are handsome and villains' looks manifest their corruption.

Horror therefore involves the demonic made visible. But the categories of horror and the demonic do not coincide. Horror includes malign forces that may not have human form at all: houses or cars that threaten and victimize their occupants, tools that take on a destructive life of their own, or animals that take us as their prey. Horror even embraces invisible dangers. On the other hand, many characters may be called *demonic* but stand outside the context of horror. Shakespeare's Caliban and Goethe's Mephistopheles are, in different ways, paradigms of the demonic. Their situations are variously magical, supernatural, and elemental, but their role is not so much to terrify us as to make us reflect on dark, barely explicable powers.

Humanizing the Demonic

Once upon a time (or so we are told by intellectual historians) persons had no trouble distinguishing themselves from God. The Old Testament tells us that God created man in His image, and Michelangelo has given us an indelible image of the event. In most religions and systems of mythology, gods have a similarly transcendental and secure existence.

From an anthropological, cultural, and secular point of view, on the other hand, persons created God. Religion and mythology are collective human inventions whose purpose is to make sense of the chaos or randomness or absurdity of existence. Psychologists suggest that God or gods are a projection, invested with human characteristics and human aspirations.

Whether man created God or gods created man matters a great deal when we try to analyze the demonic. If our cosmology includes gods, if we give them what philosophers call an independent ontological status, then we also may ask whether there are lesser gods, beings intermediate between gods and persons. In pre-Christian and non-Christian belief systems, demons were spiritual intermediaries, not necessarily identified with good or evil. Playing various roles in Greek religion, ancient Judaism, and Zoroastrianism, they could give access to special knowledge and powers. Socrates claimed that he had a *daimon* that advised him of danger and sought to guide his decisions. In some Jewish systems of demonology, demons that were approached with proper deference would explain disease and recommend cures.

The Christian Bible identifies demons with fallen angels who accompanied Lucifer when he was expelled by God from heaven. These fallen angels fell under the control of Satan. Accordingly, their sole function was to tempt persons away from obedience to God and morality. They were no longer ethically bivalent but became agents of evil.

If gods and demons are antitheses with equal claims to existence, how are we to carry out the job of imagining them? If we insist on picturing God (and thus disobey the biblical injunction to abstain from such imagemaking), we conceive of Him as an idealized person. For much of Western history, such standards of perfection were relatively uncontroversial and frequently elaborated in art. (Only in the modern era are we self-conscious about this kind of project, even to the extent of calling it parochial and discriminatory to idealize one image over another.) But how do we go about picturing the *opposite* of perfection and ideality? Imperfection, it seems, has infinitely many forms.

The art historian Germain Bazin, in his remarkable essay "The Devil in Art," reminds us that "[t]he devil, perhaps more even than God, of whom he is simply a worthless imitation, is beyond our imagining. God is one, . . . the devil is legion." Bazin quotes from the Buddhist text the *Lalitavistara* in which Mara, the devil of Tantric Buddhism, assaults the redeemer Bodhisattva, to illustrate that the devil is a matter of "[u]gliness, plurality, chaos."

> The devil . . . prepared his mighty army. . . . This army had the power to take on all manner of different appearances, transforming itself endlessly in a hundred million ways. . . . Its heads and hands and feet turned in all directions. Its eyes and faces were flaming; its stomachs, feet, and hands of all shapes. Its faces glittered in terrible splendor; its faces and teeth were of all shapes, its dog-teeth enormous, fearful to behold. Its tongues were as rough as mats of hair, its eyes red and glittering, like those of the slack serpent full of venom. Some were spitting the venom of serpents, and some, having taken the venom in their hand, were eating it. Some, like the *garudas*, having drawn out of the sea human flesh and blood, feet, hands, heads, livers, entrails and bones, were eating them. Some had bodies of flame, livid, black, bluish, red yellow; some had misshapen eyes, as hollow as empty wells, inflamed, gouged, and squinting; some had eyes that were contorted, glittering, out of shape[.] . . . Some have the ears of stags, pigs, elephants—hanging ears or boars' ears. Some have no ears at all. Some with stomachs like mountains and withered bodies made from a mass of skeleton bones, had broken noses; others had stomachs like rounded jars, feet like the feet of cranes, with skin and flesh and blood all dried up, and their ears and noses, their hands and feet, their eyes and heads all lopped off. . . . Some with the skin of oxen, asses, boars, ichneumons, stags, rams, beetles, cats, apes, wolves, and jackals, were spitting snake venom.

Bazin concludes that "[t]his fantastic accumulation of ever-changing monstrosities never manages to be more than a sum of so many parts that can never be resolved into a unity. . . . Satan creates his monsters from shattered remnants of creatures."

Western art, Bazin reminds us, has had little use for the demonic and has "centered round the search for unity, and hence for the divine, both within man and outside him." Egyptian and Greek art virtually ignored the face of the demonic. The same, with few exceptions, is true of European art. In rare flirtations with the devil, Dürer (in the engraving "The Knight, Death, and the Devil") depicts a somewhat deranged and befuddled boar, and Goya (in "The Miseries of War") a goat. Bosch, more than any Western artist in the canon, flaunts his inside knowledge of the demonic—but even here the images are relatively tame, trading on extreme deformity and dislocation of limbs (along with a scattering of insectoid demons). As Bazin observes, Chinese, other Eastern, and especially Indian culture eclipse anything Western in their vision of the demonic, a tradition that survives in Asian theatrical masks and makeup.

Writing at the onset of the Cold War, Bazin turns Cassandra with a prescient warning:

> Primitive man lived in terror of cosmic forces that were always about to be unloosed upon him. Modern man, having, thanks to science, mastered nature, has freed himself from fear. But it is a brief illusion, for now we are entering upon a time comparable with the darkest periods of human history; and we tremble with anxiety under the threat of a catastrophe whose cause no longer lies in the nature of things but in ourselves. Dispossessed of nature, his former kingdom, Lucifer now seems to have installed himself at the very center of human intelligence, which has been far too ready to put itself on a level with God, playing with the forces it has mastered without having the humility to admit that the total chain of cause and effect must always remain beyond its comprehension.

With 20/20 hindsight, we survivors of the Cold War find these warnings overwrought. But even if we have pulled away from nightmares of nuclear annihilation, the broader point remains compelling. Our deepest fears of the demonic may be fears about ourselves. Looking at advances in biology (such as cloning) and information technology, we fear that our knowledge and power may outstrip constraints of morality and responsibility. Our fear may also take a familiar psychological turn, finding evil in unconscious (or conscious) destructive aspects of human nature.

Our depiction of demons is colored by our cosmology. In this sense, it matters whether demons are given an independent existence or assumed to be figments of our imaginations and needs. In the first case we will follow the imaginative precedent of the author of the *Lalitavistara* and try to conceive of evil in effective opponents of (and antitheses of) God and angels. In the second case, we will try to picture the most thorough corruption of the human spirit, pure human malevolence.

Another way of framing the underlying philosophical quandary is whether good and evil exist in the world as organizing principles and are therefore to be found independently of human intervention and creation. Or are we the inventors and bearers of good and evil? Did we introduce these parameters to a morally indifferent world? The first possibility arises in the history of religion as gnosticism, and its most influential form is Manicheanism. The opposite view, that persons are the measure of all things, including morality, derives from the

Enlightenment and Renaissance humanism. In its extreme form, the idea of a morally indifferent world, in which our efforts to make moral sense of experience are constantly frustrated, haunts twentieth-century existentialists.

Which idea is more unsettling, a religious or mythical conviction that evil is part of the fabric of reality, or the secular view that nature is morally indifferent and that evil, such as it is, is a product of human thought and action? In both cases, evil is eternal, ineradicable. But the second possibility, demons with a human face, has the special horror of domesticating evil and thus assigning responsibility to ourselves.

These separate views of evil inspire different kinds of faces for the demonic, and it is hard to avoid speculating about the unconscious and unarticulated cosmological assumptions that guide the hands of makeup artists. Several of them, as we shall see, have filled the gap that Bazin found in Western culture by giving us memorable pictures of evil.

Hell on Earth: Vampires

We look at Hieronymus Bosch with jaded eyes. The reason so many of his demons look to us like unfortunate, if somewhat manic, persons with pitiable deformities is that horror movies have spoiled us. As horror and alien genres have crossed paths in movies and on television, effects artists have naturally fallen into "Can-you-top-this?" competitions. It is (perhaps pointlessly) debatable whether the most ingenious ways of visualizing the demonic came in the early years, with Frankenstein, Dracula, the Wolfman and their kindred. Or has there been progress, with each generation of artists building on the perverse imaginings of their forebears? However "classicists" join battle with "progressivists," there is much to savor in contemporary work, especially some little-known examples.

Most contemporary demons are capable of metamorphosis, of adopting human disguise to "pass" in the earthly world. This has a practical aspect. It saves money, time, and wear-and-tear in moviemaking if actors portraying demons do not have to be elaborately made up for every scene and, for the most part, can appear in their everyday faces. The demons that seem to have assimilated best to the task of passing as humans are generally vampires. In the last decade, vampires have had a renaissance, in literature as well as in movies and TV.

Why vampires? A simple psychological explanation is reasonably plausible. The characteristic moral and political preoccupation at century's end is to redefine individuality, identity, and privacy. We fear, in other words, our lifeblood (that is, our identity) being drained, both by what we discover in reassessing the past and what we fear in our collective future.

For example, feminism, gay rights, and multiculturalism are all ways of making the claim that groups (women, homosexuals, minorities) have been denied their "voice" and their identity through discrimination. At the same time, efforts to rectify such harms through reverse discrimination or prohibitions on hate speech are seen as ways of restricting what other persons can do and are attacked as constraints on freedom. Beyond all this, technology threatens to invade our privacy and even our sense of identity. Computers can monitor our behavior, giving strangers unlimited access to our lives, and imposters in cyberspace can, more easily than ever, pretend to be us. Protecting our cultural and personal lifeblood from all forms of vampirism calls for unnatural vigilance.

Vampirism has its advantages, principally immortality. While other demons may enjoy preying on human beings, vampires *need* to do so. They are sustained by human blood, and their human victims either die or become vampires themselves (usually at the discretion of the author/screenwriter). Thus even though vampires are demons and not human, the border is highly permeable, even if traffic is, for the most part, one-way.

Perhaps the fact that most vampires are ex-humans explains how easily they can assume a human guise. Their true appearance, on the other hand, should terrify us every bit as much as their revealed intentions do. Makeup artists can take a minimalist or a maximalist approach to such designs. A maximalist artist remakes the actor from stem to stern, typically using a rubber body suit. Every hideous feature should terrify and testify to their evil. The minimalist, on the other hand, is convinced that fangs, a pulsating brow, and penetrating yellow eyes are enough to convey the vampire's nature.

KNB, a studio founded by Bob Kurtzman, Greg Nicotero, and Howard Berger, takes all kinds of makeup challenges but is best known for horror and "creatures." Its vampires for *From Dusk Till Dawn* are extravagant rococo monstrosities, both state of the art and over the top. They approach the point at which sheer horror becomes deliberate mockery of the genre. These monsters deconstruct horror as much as they embody it. We are moved to cower and at the same time to laugh at ourselves for cowering. None of this is surprising in a movie written by (and featuring) Quentin Tarantino, with Robert Rodriguez directing.

The plot is a wind-up toy which culminates in a dead-of-night end-of-the-world encounter in a Mexican casino/pleasure palace between the resourceful but hapless protagonists, played by Juliette Lewis and George Clooney, and the local denizens, virtually all of whom reveal themselves as demons and vampires opportunistically camouflaged as human. Animatronics, computer morphing effects, and prosthetic makeup appliances are used in every possible combination to convince us that nothing is what it seems, and everything is more sinister and awful than we can imagine.

Figure 4.1. A collection of vampire-demons from *From Dusk Till Dawn*. Makeup by KNB Studios.

Figures 4.2, 4.3. Two demons from *From Dusk Till Dawn*, thirsty for blood. Makeup by KNB Studios.

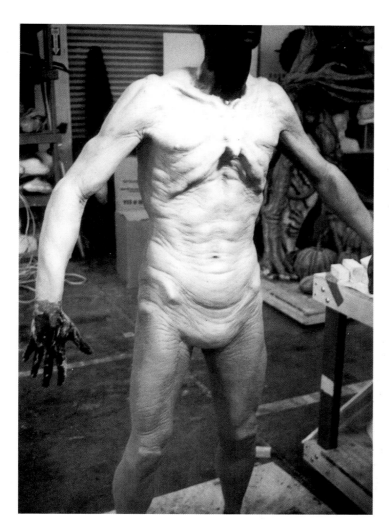

Figure 4.4. A rubber bodysuit for a *From Dusk Till Dawn* demon. Makeup by KNB Studios.

But the pièce de résistance is KNB's use of persons in rubber suits. The challenge is obviously improbable, to create creatures that are profoundly hideous, mindlessly threatening, and profoundly silly. Although countless members of the cast and crew took turns appearing in various monstrous guises, only a few characters were executed in loving detail, the kind that does not give its artificiality away when the camera lingers. (The dark secret of many extreme makeups—and this goes for animatronic creatures and rubber prosthetics equally—is the importance of the fleeting glimpse.)

In *From Dusk Till Dawn* a handful of creatures withstands scrutiny. Here illusion is sustained. The deformations, both of body and head, seem too great. The deformed muscles, the distended flesh, and the protruding skeleton are such that we suspend awareness of the normal-looking actor beneath. The faces work hyperbolic variations on the most fearsome animalistic features: canine teeth, the furrowed snout, inhuman pinpoint eyes, and grossly stretched skin over a bulbous and misshaped cranium.

Producing and wearing the suit is, not surprisingly, an ordeal for actors and makeup artists alike. First of all, unwieldy molds of the actor's entire body are needed. The suit is sculpted on a lifesize replica of the actor. The production of the rubber suit follows the same steps as the creation of facial appliances, but the positive and negative casts are massive, awkward plaster molds. Viscous liquid latex is injected between the positive mold of the actor's body and the negative mold of the demonic sculpture. Special gargantuan ovens are usually needed to "cure" the rubber. The rubber suit fits the actor's body like an added skin. Typically it is fragile and requires continuous maintenance and repair.

It is also torturous to wear. The zipper that allows the actor to enter the suit may by buried in sealants. The one-piece suit itself may have no openings; wearing the suit for an extended day on the set, perhaps as long as sixteen hours, the actor inside the suit may have limited or no opportunities to perform basic bodily functions. Remarkable feats of continence are more than myth. Beyond all this, wearing the suit plays havoc with other normal bodily needs. Actors can barely hear or see through the suits, they lack the ability to touch and feel, and the suit can cause body temperature to destabilize. It may be easy for actors thus encumbered to become homicidally demonic in reality.

Lower budgets, sympathy for actors, and an austere esthetic produce a more modest approach to creating vampires. For the TV series *Tales from the Crypt*, Todd Masters turned Walter Phelan and Josh Patton (who also wore the stem-to-stern rubber suits in *From Dusk Till Dawn*) into vampires with a reptilian aspect. Yellow eyes, a beetled brow, and a permanent snarl complement the obligatory pointed incisors that allow these vampires to perform their essential functions.

A similar concept, even closer to minimalism, is used by John Vulich in the designs for vampires in the television adaptation of *Buffy the Vampire Slayer*. As horror-comedy, *Buffy*, like *From Dusk Till Dawn*, melds and tampers with traditional categories. Both mock melodramatic appeals to emotion and dare us to take them (or our reponses) seriously. Both deconstruct the conventions of horror, but *Buffy* does so with a lighter touch. Becoming a *Buffy* vampire is again a matter of teeth and eyes, along with pulsating brows and sharpened cheekbones. The appliances, crafted by Vulich's Optic Nerve Studios and applied on-set by Todd McIntosh and his team, never mask the character's human identity as they efficiently add essential malice.

The *Buffy* conception of vampireness reached something of an apogee in the

Figure 4.5. Walter Phelan

Figure 4.6. Josh Patton

Figure 4.7. *Left* Walter Phelan and *right* Josh Patton incarnate a pair of *Tales from the Crypt* demons. Makeup by Todd Masters/MastersFX.

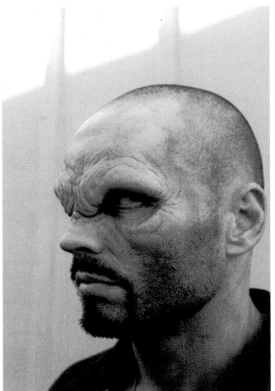

Figures 4.8, 4.9, 4.10, 4.11, 4.12, 4.13. A collection of vampires and demons for *Buffy the Vampire Slayer* (TV). Makeup designed by artists associated with Optic Nerve Studios; applied by Todd McIntosh's team of makeup artists.

59

character of the Master, played by Mark Metcalf. The character is dessicated, consumed with its own malevolence. He stands somewhere between playful evil—malevolence lite with an accompanying touch of transformative makeup—and the unredeemable weight of go-for-broke evil as in *From Dusk Till Dawn*. And his makeup is, to that extent, heavier and at a farther distance from anything human.

Figure 4.14. Mark Metcalf

The Pure Demonic

Vampires never quite lose their link to humanity. In this sense they are tragic as much as demonic. Their origins are human, and they survive by maintaining human ties, by drinking the lifeblood of humans. Immortality has its price.

Pure demons, on the other hand, have no such weakness or dependence. Just as God can presumably exist without man (just as the Creation was optional rather than necessary), so too can Satan exist without persons. A demon's life is just duller without persons to prey upon, a life that has lost its raison d'être.

There are many strategies for meeting Bazin's challenge of visualizing the pure demonic. Two avenues are interesting, but offer little employment for makeup artists. One of these is to assume that Satan or demons look just like us. Mephistopheles in *Faust* and the title character in *The Devil and Daniel Webster* transact the business of buying and selling souls, or otherwise making life systematically miserable, in human guise. Looking human is not merely advantageous to devils themselves. It also helps the writer explain how easily the victims fall under a devil's spell. By contrast, when the appearance of devils or demons consistently alerts the world to their nature, plot possibilities are drastically limited.

A different approach is openly metaphorical. The demonic may be embodied in a creature with a mundane aspect. The white whale in *Moby Dick* is a plausible metaphor for the demonic, but it remains ambiguous. Similarly, animals *(Cujo)* and even buildings *(The Shining)* can stand for the demonic, crossing the border between fact and metaphor.

It is not the job of transformational makeup artists to create normal-looking

Figure 4.15. Mark Metcalf becomes the Master on *Buffy the Vampire Slayer*. Makeup by Optic Nerve Studios; applied by Todd McIntosh and associates.

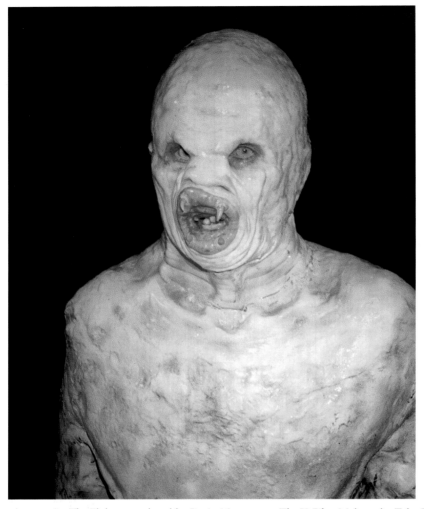

Figure 4.16. The Flukeman, played by Darin Morgan, on *The X-Files*. Makeup by Toby Lindala.

actors or equally normal-looking whales. Their concern is not with entities that *are* demonic in ways *belied* by their looks, but rather with creatures that *look* demonic. So Bazin's dilemma, that the demonic has no distinctive look, remains.

A partial solution is situational. Certain creatures, arising out of peculiar and awesome circumstances, are purely malevolent with no mix of humanity. A particularly rebarbative example from *The X-Files* has the unassuming name of Flukeman. He is an omnivorous beast that, raised in radioactive water, is biologically a fluke (defined as a "trematode that feeds on humans," in other words a primitive worm-like parasite) but has grown from his normal near-microscopic size to human dimensions. (One hopes the pun is intentional.)

Flukeman is a man-in-a-suit. In this case, the suit is diabolically uncomfort-

Figure 4.17. Vincent D'Onofrio

Figure 4.18. Rick Baker's makeup for *Men in Black* turns Vincent D'Onofrio into a malevolent alien inhabiting the deteriorating body of a farmer.

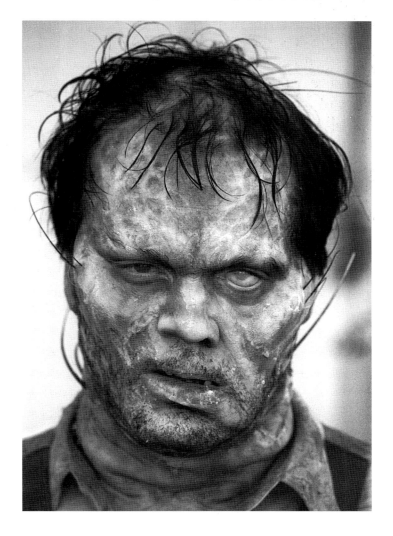

Figure 4.19. Alan Shockley-Gray

Figure 4.20. Alan Shockley-Gray wears vampire makeup originally designed for *The Lost Boys*. Makeup by Steve Johnson/XFX Inc.

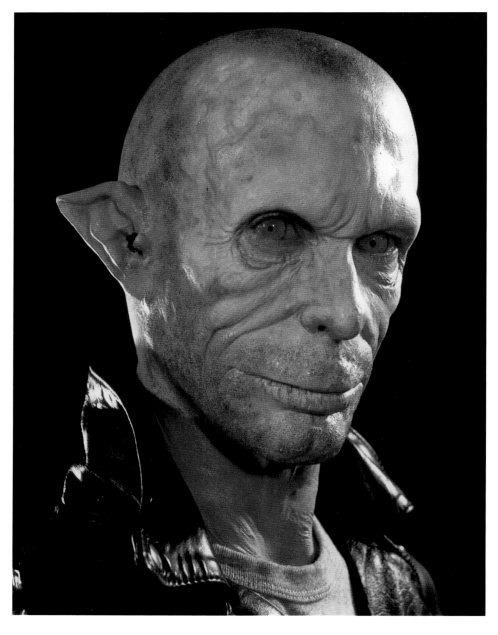

able, denying the actor normal use of his limbs, normal head movement, and so on. The production of the suit, however, is simpler than those in *From Dusk Till Dawn*, much less detailed and not formfitting. The actor, Darin Morgan, has also been the writer of several *X-Files* episodes, and one must assume he was an eager and willing collaborator in his own torture. The image of Flukeman is a particularly disconcerting version of the demonic, calling up neither the cunning of animals or reptiles but a creature far more primitive than either.

Another image of the demonic as it arises in special circumstances is the character played by Vincent D'Onofrio in the movie *Men in Black*. D'Onofrio is a farmer whose body is slowly and inexorably taken over by a malevolent alien. As the body is corrupted, it deteriorates and takes an alien form. The special charm of *Men in Black* is its celebration of the endless variety of aliens, benign and evil, obtuse and cunning, vertebrate and invertebrate, microscopic and threateningly large. Rick Baker's team at Cinovation Studios set out its smorgasbord of aliens with a grab bag of state-of-the-art techniques: men in suits, animatronics, computer simulations, and other tools. The D'Onofrio alien is the closest they come to a purely demonic character.

Neither Flukeman nor the creature from *Men in Black* represents pure, noncontextual evil. None of the images we have looked at so far does this. Vampires are defined by their dependence on humans. Other demons are produced by special conditions which determine their countenance. Bazin, as we saw, defies us to imagine the pure demonic. Over the history of art, we have had our shots at picturing godlike ideality. But what images reveal absolute nonideality, absolute evil and malevolence?

The ranks of transformational makeup artists offer up a candidate to meet the challenge. Steve Johnson, founder and head of XFX Inc., has a gift for the diabolical. Time and time again, he has conjured up demons that threaten to do for the contemporary imagination what Bosch did for the late fifteenth century. And some of his best designs are little known.

The 1987 horror-satire movie *The Lost Boys* is about vampires. The makeup actually used to transform Jason Patric, Kiefer Sutherland, and their coven was devised by Greg Cannom. It was a minimal transformation, a design that influenced the makeup design on *Buffy the Vampire Slayer*. Steve Johnson's losing bid for the makeup work on *Lost Boys* was much more elaborate, a set of prosthetic appliances that fully covered and contorted the actor's head. The image went beyond the suggestion of vampirism to an image of pure evil.

This particular makeup has had a shadow life, known mostly to aficionados. The makeup, as photographed, is not modeled by an actor at all, but by Alan Shockley-Gray, who was Johnson's office and business manager. The pieces were not designed with Gray in mind, but were nevertheless a near-perfect fit.

Figure 4.21. T. Ryder Smith

Figure 4.22. The Trickster, the evil demon of a computer, is played by T. Ryder Smith in *Brainscan*. Makeup by Steve Johnson/XFX Inc.

For the movie *Brainscan*, Steve Johnson transformed T. Ryder Smith into the Trickster, a character that erupts from a computer program to enslave the teenage user's mind and body. The movie traded on our apprehension about computer technology, and the Trickster could be seen as the most lethal and embodied of computer viruses. But, ironically, he hardly looked the part of an emissary from the future. He combined the demeanor and dress of an Edwardian fop with a leering and diabolical visage, unmistakably a lineal descendent of the demon design for *The Lost Boys*.

Johnson's special flair for demons emerged early. Even in high school, he turned friends into creatures of darkness. At least one tantalizing photo survives from that time.

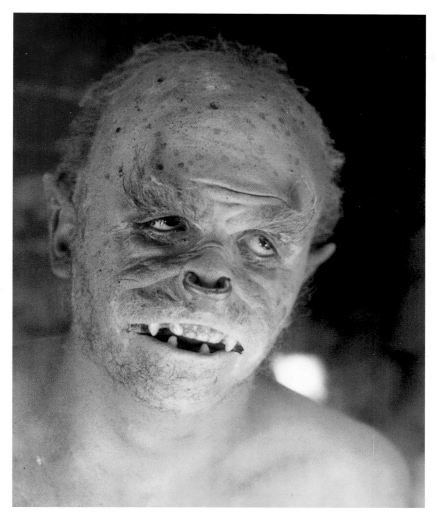

Figure 4.23. Steve Johnson transformed a high school friend for Halloween.

All of Steve Johnson's demons veer aggressively away from anything human, although it is hard, especially with the Trickster, to pinpoint the features that confirm our horror. A particularly elegant, if simpler, demon makeup by Todd McIntosh for the television series *V.R.5* identifies the common denominator of a vision of the demonic. If the character lacks horns, at least it has the beetled brow, the deepset eyes, and the probing and pointy nose and chin that make up the "lean and hungry look" of pure evil.

John Vulich's Optic Nerve Studios summed up our image of demons in an intimidating makeup that was barely used in *The X-Files*. Brian Blair, one of the makeup artists responsible for *The X-Files*, wore the makeup. Except for the glowering eyes, the individual features of this demon are human. The total ef-

Figures 4.24, 4.25, 4.26, 4.27. The stages of a demonic transformation by Todd McIntosh for the television series *V.R.5*.

The Practice of Transformation

Figure 4.28. Brian Blair

Figure 4.29. His fellow makeup artists at Optic Nerve turned Brian Blair into a demon for *The X-Files*.

fect, however, is more than the sum of its parts. The look is timelessly demonic, drawing inspiration from medieval art as much as contemporary fantasy.

Demons Within

Whether or not they masquerade as human, the demons we have looked at so far are not persons. They belong to (nether)worlds outside. They meld the natural with the supernatural. Just as religion invests the natural world with supernatural powers that give life meaning and grace, these demons invest the natural with transcendent powers that promise to annihilate us.

Many persons of a secular bent reject such a metaphysics. They believe that good and evil, grace and innate corruption are concepts that persons bring to a morally indifferent natural world. Psychologists speak about projection and externalization of moral categories. They show how this can occur on both personal and cultural levels. Gods and demons are, on this view, our hopes, fears, and ideals writ large and incarnated.

If evil is within us, if we are its source as well as its victims, then demons wear human faces. More often than not, stories about evil-with-a-human-face presuppose that one cannot tell much from appearances. Human demons look just like us. Only their behavior shows them to be terrorists, mass murderers, psychopaths, or sadists.

But we also fear certain kinds of inevitable human predicaments that have distinctive physical marks. And these fears inspire a sense of the demonic that is palpable and visible, and that has little to do with the supernatural. These fears are the universal fears of death and disease. Each in its own way gives rise to fierce ambivalence.

We acknowledge that death is necessary to give life meaning. The predicament of vampires, who have eternal life, is eternal and terminal boredom. The certainty of death gives life urgency and prompts us to give it a shape, a trajectory. But most of us would put off death as long as we can; if possible, forever. Thus, we both reject and embrace immortality. We are similarly ambivalent toward the possibility of life after death. While Christianity and other religions see life on earth as mere preparation for the hereafter and celebrate the possibility of eternal bliss, the earthly immortals who survive death in fiction become the undead, desperately malcontent zombies who take mortals as their prey. We saw in Chapter 2 that the capacity to evade mortality is both a blessing and a curse.

Our attitudes toward deformity are also ambivalent. Bosch's demons were deformed. We like to think that we live in an enlightened era in which we no longer fear the deformed, and we emphasize the need to undercut stereotypes and feel empathy toward all fellow beings. But the disabled themselves are the first to remind us that our moral impulses and visceral responses are rarely in harmony.

When makeup artists create demons, their template is our fears rather than our moral impulses. Two categories of horror are the undead and the barely human. Both categories exploit the fine line between fear and pity, and between pity for ourselves as victims and as possible perpetrators of horror. Seeing the undead and deformed we can hardly help thinking, "There but for grace go I."

It does not take an extravagant imagination to call up the undead. Fleshly deterioration is all too common, even if it is generally hidden from squeamish sensibilities. One way of depicting the undead is of a skeletal face, with decaying flesh barely stretched over an emergent skull. Typically (as in the *Dead* Trilogy:

Night of the Living Dead, Dawn of the Dead, Day of the Dead) this is accomplished by building up the actor's eyesockets, adding patches of deteriorating skin, and making false teeth visible in a disintegrating mouth.

Gabe Bartalos' makeup on Robert Rusler for *Sometimes They Come Back* plays variations on the theme of the undead. Decay and collapse of the cranial structure are well advanced. Even if the undead are said to be immortal, *this* character is disintegrating so fast that he hardly seems long for the world of zombies.

Figure 4.30. Robert Rusler

Figures 4.31, 4.32 (this page), **4.33, 4.34** (page 72). Robert Rusler became a zombie in *Sometimes They Come Back*. Makeup by Gabe Bartalos/Atlantic West Effects.

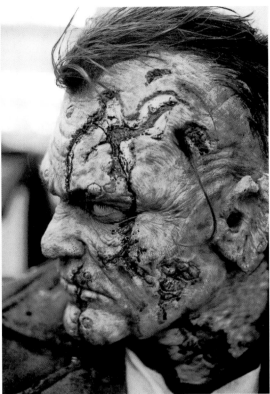

More troubling than any preoccupation with the undead is a concern with the deformed. In "Home," a controversial episode of *The X-Files*, the FBI agents Mulder and Scully confront a crime wave traceable to a rural family of near-monstrous recluses, ironically named the Peacocks. Incest in the family produces three brothers who are severely retarded and deformed. (One brother is said to be the parent of the other two, so in fact they are half-brothers.) Their homicidal behavior is unthinking, instinctive. It can be seen merely as territorial and self-protective. And yet the Peacocks are creatures of horror as much as they are objects of pity.

In designing the makeup for the Peacocks, Toby Lindala studied medical texts on cranial deformation associated with retardation. His efforts tap into the ambiguity of any attempt to bridge the human and the demonic, to find the human *in* the demonic. In part the issue is one of responsibility. We lose our way when we ask whether the Peacocks deserve more blame than pity and whether they can be held to account for their conduct.

The question hardly arises with gods and demons that have no part in humanity and are part of the cosmological order. Choice and responsibility are char-

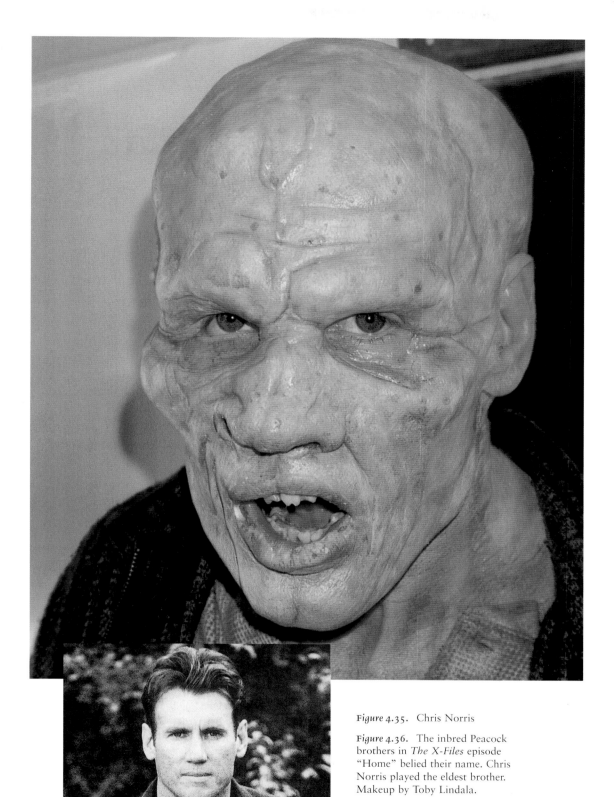

Figure 4.35. Chris Norris

Figure 4.36. The inbred Peacock brothers in *The X-Files* episode "Home" belied their name. Chris Norris played the eldest brother. Makeup by Toby Lindala.

Figure 4.37. Jonathan Fuller

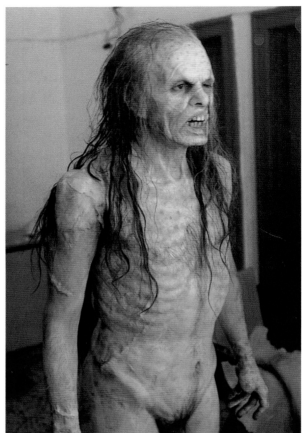

Figures 4.38, 4.39. Jonathan Fuller as he appeared in the title role as *Castle Freak*. Makeup by John Vulich/Optic Nerve.

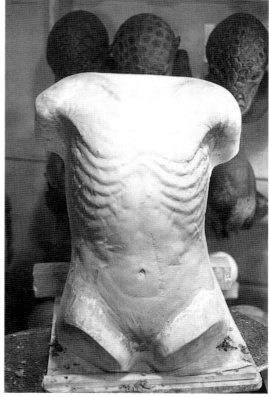

Figures 4.40, 4.41. Optic Nerve's face and body sculptures for *Castle Freak*.

Figure 4.42. Jonathan Fuller poses in unpainted prosthetics for *Castle Freak*.

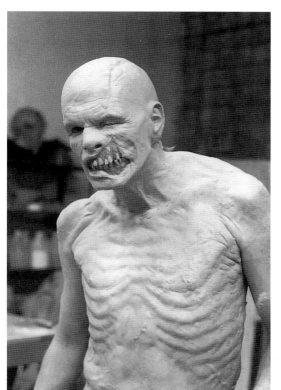

acteristics of persons; gods and demons act because of their nature, not their freedom. But with persons—*all* persons—the question of free will is a continuing co-
nundrum. Philosophers try to explain how it is that we all, obviously, act on the
basis of our nature (our histories, expectations, opinions, goals) and at the same
time can be said to act freely and responsibly. Some philosophers have argued
that freedom is an illusion. Among those who have thought so, some have taken
comfort in this conclusion and others have found it unacceptably troubling.

The situation of those who are marginally responsible and yet demonically
evil is much more than the stuff of horror. We pity the Peacock brothers (or the
Frankenstein monster) as we cannot pity the vampires of *Dusk Till Dawn* or
Buffy. Our pity, our recognition of their humanity, makes them more, not less,
frightening.

John Vulich's creature from the movie *Castle Freak* stretches the limits of horror even more than the Peacocks. Here again the design of the creature gets a
more complex response than the story itself warrants. The creature has grown
up in captivity, has spent its life chained in the dank cellar of a castle. It is barely
self-aware and hardly able to have thoughts or intentions. Like the Frankenstein
monster, its destructive actions are not predatory. It is newly freed and exploring
a world in which a creature so deformed and deprived seems to have no place.

Vulich gives us a scarred and torn creature, crippled by its desperate efforts to
escape. Its mouth is largely chewed away. Prosthetic appliances over most of the
actor's (Jonathan Fuller) head and body give him a wasted body and ravaged
face. The demonic, it seems, is here fully humanized but loses none of its power
to shock.

On Fear

Demons are serious business, the business of fear. Imagining the demonic is the
job of embodying our fears, in particular fear of what we cannot control. Psychologists tell us that the external demons that terrorize us are often projections,
fears of our own impulses, wishes, and capacities, fears of what we cannot control in ourselves. If that is true, then the makeup artists' vampires, zombies, and
grotesques are mirrors. Recognizing this, we find our identity in these transformations just as we exorcise fear by indulging it.

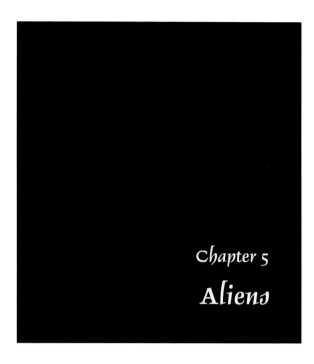

Chapter 5

Aliens

On doit se regarder soi-meme un fort long temps,
Avant que de songer a condamner les gens.

(One should give oneself a long, hard look
before thinking of passing judgment on others.)

MOLIÈRE, *Le Misanthrope*

The Humanity of Aliens

Alien simply means "other," presumably anyone not one's self. But it is linguistically odd to refer to your friends or even strangers indiscriminately as "aliens" unless you are being ironic, sarcastic, or just plain nasty. In less nuanced usage, the term refers to other nationalities, but not ordinarily to other ethnic groups or races. Used in these latter contexts, it carries controversial implications of separation, denigration, and rejection. Except as a way of distinguishing nationalities, the term has negative, literally divisive, connotations.

Of course, aliens are also beings from other planets, perhaps other galaxies—

extraterrestrials. Since most of us see it as at best an open question whether sentient beings exist elsewhere than on Earth, such aliens are the stuff of fiction. But we are mindful that fiction may any day become fact.

If there are sentient aliens, how do they look? Common sense and scientific theory both afford little reason to think of aliens as near human in appearance or capacities. Their senses, their ways of sustaining life, their motive powers, and their modes of communication and procreation are quite unguessable. They might be more like what we know as lobsters, coral, or bacteria than like animals or humans. They might even come in clusters of cells without meeting any obvious criteria for individuating one creature from another; distinguishing a particular entity might be arbitrary.

When science fiction writers write scripts, their imaginations are constrained by plot possibilities. The dramatic possibilities involving large amoebae or alien coral are limited. They might exude lethal poisons. They might proliferate like crazy. They might look *really* ugly, robbing onlookers of their sanity or turning them to stone. Otherwise, what?

Aliens that are not remotely human present two very different kinds of challenges. Aside from story limitations, there are technical and practical ones. The creatures must be brought to life through conventional animation, simulated and manipulated by computer animation, or created as sophisticated puppets in three dimensions through animatronics. All three techniques may be used in a single project.

Even with the technical advances of the last two decades, these three methods of creature creation remain expensive, time-consuming, painstaking, and restricted in what they can achieve. An animated image, whether it is Elmer Fudd or the villain in *Terminator 2*, must still be designed and choreographed frame by frame. Computers have seductive but circumscribed uses. They can effect smooth transitions between invented images, whether they involve "morphing" one human being into another, a person into a quicksilver or transparently liquid version of himself, the separation of an intact person into a discrete collection of separated body parts, or merely a transition that mimics motion from one position to another. They can make a cat or a dinosaur or President Nixon appear to say things they never said, manipulating images of moving lips and simulating expressions. Moreover, animatronic faces and creatures can, to the extent that the complex servo-machinery under the fake skin allows, appear to move, talk, and emote.

Nonetheless, creatures evoked in all of these ways cannot now move, talk, act, and respond with anything like the versatility and ease of real actors. In even the most sophisticated recent projects, the manipulation of images remains a kind of stunt. The talking, smiling, and scowling reindeer in *The Santa Clause*, the out-of-control changes in body shape or size of Eddie Murphy in *The Nutty Professor* and Jim Carrey in *The Mask*, and the reinvention of historical events in *Forrest Gump* all involve momentary visual tricks. They remain various ingenious hybrids of cartoon and reality, not much more convincingly real than *Who Framed Roger Rabbit?*

These techniques may eventually allow us to dispense with actors. We may eventually be able to create and manipulate the image of a person in an infinite array of settings and situations efficiently and cheaply. We may, in other words, be able to produce all that we now see on the screen without putting actual actors or objects in front of a camera at all. Just as we might be able to simulate the sounds of an orchestra electronically without resorting to real instruments, we might thus simulate every aspect of "real" filmed scenes entirely by manipulating artificial images and sounds. Moviemaking as we know it would become obsolete.

We are not there yet. And we may be far from that not-so-brave new world. It is important not only to appreciate the gap between current resources and these fantasies but also to consider how such changes would affect our experience of movies. The fact that a technique is possible or available does not make it desirable. It is probable that we go to movies in large part because we want to see real people acting. To know that an actor is a computer-manipulated image may be no less disconcerting than discovering that a trusted friend and colleague is a robot. The point of having computer-enhanced and computer-created creatures participating in situations from *Star Wars* to *Forrest Gump* is that they enhance a human predicament enacted by human actors. Just possibly, if the central actors were also computer-created, the entire dramatic exercise might lose its point. At the very least, it would be transformed to the level of involvement we accord cartoons.

Technological limitations are hardly the main reason why alien beings as represented in movies and TV are suspiciously humanoid. A more important reason is that the range of plots that might involve giant amoebas, microscopic or invisible aliens, shape-shifters, and monstrous replicants as in the *Alien* movies is narrow. They can be a threat or a boon to human welfare. Once their orientation is made clear the plot is likely to unfold with deadly predictability.

In other words, most interesting plots—interesting to humans, if not to aliens—are about human transactions, about the complex emotions and reflections that are intrinsic to intercourse with other persons. The alienness of nonhumanoids is, therefore, best exploited by anecdotes, story fragments that glimpse experience rather than contemplate it. The anecdotes of the old TV series *The Twilight Zone* are thus sometimes able to exploit the experience of alienness as not-at-all-human. The somewhat longer form of a two-hour movie—consider *Alien* or *The Thing*—

can sustain an encounter with nonhumanoid aliens, but only by distracting us with dramatic tensions among the human characters.

When we move to an even longer form, ongoing TV series such as *Star Trek* in its many iterations, or *Babylon 5*, the scriptwriters' Hobson's choice is all too clear. They can stick with aliens in all their barely imaginable alienness and run out of plots after a handful of episodes. Or they turn them into humanoids and reimagine the entire catalog of plots that have informed non-science-fiction theater and movies from their start. Add the fact that the more human an alien is the less one has to rely on complex and expensive special visual effects, and it becomes obvious why aliens are often all too human.

Metaphors Rampant

Stories involving aliens—humanoid or not, but extraterrestrial for the most part—are pigeonholed as science fiction. The term "science fiction" alludes to a shotgun wedding lurching toward divorce. The demands of the two disciplines conflict. Science, especially scientific discovery, may have its own inherent drama, but the excitement of discovery and invention primarily infects participants rather than audiences. The characteristic emotions and interactions of research scientists rarely make for gripping fiction. And the major discoveries of science usually earn a two-minute sound bite and three column inches on an inside page. Serial killers get more respect.

Of course, some scientific hypotheses stir up fictional imaginings. Einsteinian reflections on time, energy, and motion revived speculation about time travel. Our knowledge of exotic viruses inspires terror scenarios of unmanageable epidemics. And the reality of space travel allows us to speculate about such likely predicaments as colonizing other planets and being lost in space.

But even these scenarios are quickly exhausted. *Fiction* remains the dominant partner in the cohabitation of science and fiction. Aliens with a humanoid countenance are not just evidence of the scientific half-heartedness of science fiction. They also suggest that the science in science fiction is sometimes just a pretext. Outer space, the distant future, and encounters with other civilizations may simply constitute an arena in which storytellers can explore themes transposed from the familiar present world, themes that they can examine more freely and less threateningly in camouflage.

In general, culture often comes in code. One way in which art historians intimidate lay readers is by demonstrating that paintings are often designed in code. The objects that surround the Christ child in a medieval tableau or the household effects in a Dutch interior from the Golden Age are not chosen randomly merely for esthetic impact. They are symbols, and their symbolic weight is dictated by a code known to most educated contemporaries of the artist, one that has survived largely in the esoterica of scholarly experts.

The use of codes is not limited to classical painting, of course. Novels and other works of art produced in circumstances of political repression are often written in code, again one that is well understood internally. Solzhenitsyn's *The Cancer Ward* is said to be about the social malaise of Soviet society, not literally about a cancer ward. George Orwell's *1984* and *Animal Farm* are examinations of totalitarianism in our own time rather than imaginative forays into possible futures and impossible barnyards.

The use of codes is the sign of a relatively closed and homogeneous society, one in which all who experience the work of art have the relevant keys. Coded art in this sense may be obsolete to the extent that we no longer have the educational, religious, and cultural resources that guarantee a shared frame of reference. Aspiring to be so-called multiculturalists, we are sometimes said to be troubled by any reliance on a shared canon of cultural works. And the existence and familiarity of a canon seems to be a prerequisite for the use of codes.

We can distinguish codes from metaphors. When a code is needed to decipher a work of art (a painting, a novel) it is a mistake, a failing caused by naivete, to take the work at face value. But when the work is an extended metaphor, it can be taken at several levels that complement and illuminate each other. A naive reading is not a mistake, but it is incomplete.

Resorting to metaphor may or may not be a response to repression. But it is often dictated by the need to say indirectly what cannot or should not be said directly. The most obvious situation is repression, a political context in which free expression is punished, in which dissent and unpopular opinions are criminalized. The sanctions are more commonly informal. The last fifteen years have spawned controversy about the social practice of monitoring speech and behavior for what is called political correctness. Perhaps *moral correctness* is a better term; moral criticism and moral censure are the core of such debates. Even when sanctions are not the main concern, moral, political, and social questions may best be addressed indirectly. Emotionally charged issues may be defused by indirection, and metaphors are the standard literary strategy for doing so.

Humanoid aliens are perfect surrogates for other races, religions, ethnicities, and nationalities. Political and social conflict over human history typically takes the form of an "us against them" situation, and the human confrontation with aliens is the ultimate "us against them" story. Arguably, a political commitment to humanism and egalitarianism has put to rest some questions about what to believe about those with whom we do not share race, religion, or cultural background, and about how to act. But humanism and egalitarianism are hardly universal; internationally they remain more the exception than the rule. And in every culture that claims to adhere to these principles as ideals, many individuals and groups remain skeptical and regularly reject them through their words and acts.

It is natural to fear what we do not know. It is also natural to try to rationalize and justify our fears by discovering or inventing "facts." And we generally do not know persons who have different backgrounds. Calls for unreserved acceptance of others fly in the face of these instinctual, if sometimes regrettable, aspects of experience.

Fear and mistrust of aliens colors the opening gambit of any story involving extraterrestrials. If the fear is justified, if they are simply malevolent (as in the *Alien* movies), the drama becomes a basic confrontation of good and evil and of self-preservation in the face of danger. If the aliens have enough guile to seem benign and to seduce us into accepting them, the confrontation is merely delayed. But all such stories tacitly prey upon our fears: those who are not like us are not to be trusted.

Usually the situation is more tangled. Mistrust may be out of place if the aliens are not committed to subversion, conquest, or destruction. But how much should we fraternize and how should we regard them? What dangers does fraternization present? Can we enslave, dominate, and rule them? Can we colonize them in the interest of sharing our "superior" history, culture, and dispositions with them? Can we coexist peacefully?

Even if we refrain from replaying the mistakes of nineteenth-century imperial history (and we may even second-guess our reasons for calling them "mistakes"), how should we think of aliens? By what criteria should we measure their culture and attitudes against our own, or judge them to be our inferiors, peers, or even superiors? If they eat each other, avoid treating the sick, procreate without sex, and revere earthworms, how should we look at these practices? What tools do we have for even *understanding* them? Should they have political rights and privileges and be treated socially and politically as our equals—regardless of their beliefs and practices? To what extent should we refrain from generalizing about aliens and shape our attitudes by what we learn about particular groups, particular individuals? If we "should," can we?

These political and social questions bring moral and esthetic dilemmas in their wake. How should we decide whether to interact—and how should we judge those fellow humans who do? Do moral obligations extend to aliens? Which moral obligations? Do our obligations extend to our attitudes as well as our actions? Are our attitudes subject to our will?

If the aliens have bulbous heads or lack noses, have several mouths or iridescent scaly skin, how do we adjust our esthetic standards? Even if we are "politically correct" and refrain from judging them, may we concede that we find them ugly or beautiful or that we have trouble telling them apart? What is involved in applying our standards of beauty to alien races? Can we form appropriate standards—and find some of them handsome, others not? Can we inhabit the criteria they use themselves?

Every politically sensitive question about the otherness of other persons has a possible analog in a story about aliens. Aliens can be a metaphor for women or for gay persons, for the handicapped or the eccentric, for the saint in a world of sinners or the sinner in a world of saints. The problem with stories about humanoid aliens, therefore, is not that they are a specialized genre, limited by what is scientifically imaginable, but that they potentially embrace every possible situation of otherness, a category without shape or limits.

The makeup artist's job, however, is to *visualize* aliens and create them. He has a kind of freedom that more ordinary dramatic situations do not afford. We know what blacks, Asians, women, children, and French men look like. We know that gay persons look just like heterosexuals. The makeup artist questions these facts at his peril. But we don't know what aliens look like, and we do know that we can hardly ask scientists for much help.

So the makeup artist has choices. He can make their appearance a reflection of their nature, their history, their morality, their practices. Or he can do the opposite and create an appearance that belies their true nature, forcing us to discover what they are *in spite* of their looks. Or he can do neither and simply give free rein to his imagination.

Thus, the makeup artist is forced to consider a question that is deeply puzzling, deeply disputed. Is Orwell right, and do our faces come to reflect our natures, to betray who and what we are? Or are faces masks that fool the world into accepting a false persona? Is Shakespeare right that a "lean and hungry look" reliably mirrors a calculating nature that we trust at our peril? Or are we to avoid such judgments as prejudicial and based on flawed assumptions?

If we persist in tracking the relevant contemporary moral climate on this question (and we will not), we may again bump our heads against controversy. We have already seen that it seems instinctive to fear what we do not know—and yet it is arguably morally incumbent on us to embrace persons with other practices and beliefs, and perhaps with prejudices of their own. We have seen that judgments about beauty and handsomeness are also instinctive—and also suspect. The same can be said, the same dilemma haunts us, when we entertain the idea that we must judge others by appearance because appearance "often makes the man." Does it?

In any case, the makeup artist must give the alien *some* look. And the temptation to correlate appearance with other characteristics—either in a mirroring or antithetical relationship—is just about irresistible.

Deeper into Aliens

Although *The Good, the Bad, and the Ugly* was a Sergio Leone spaghetti western, it has one of the more inspired and adaptable titles of all time. The three categories neatly fit the basic characteristics a screenwriter and a makeup artist must identify in designing aliens. But the categories are not mutually exclusive; the good or the bad will often be ugly as well—ugly, that is, to human eyes.

The good and the bad are correlated, roughly and imperfectly, with the superhuman and the subhuman. The genealogy of good aliens leads back to mythology and religion. Gods were, more often than not, superhuman beings who chose to involve themselves in human affairs. In primitive cosmology, they often dwelled outside the time and space parameters of human habitation. They resisted visualization. Greeks gods assumed human form for the temporary purpose of having intercourse, verbal and other, with humans. In Buddhist theology, the ground of all being is ineffable. In the Old Testament, man is forbidden to reduce God to graven images. The God of Christianity is characteristically conceived by artists as a perfected human.

Movies conceptualize *really good* aliens along similar lines. Religion inspires the imagery of movies from *2001: A Space Odyssey* to *Contact*. In both stories, superhuman and superterrestrial powers are responsible for the progress of mankind and its domination of nature. In *2001* those powers are represented by omnipresent, mysterious monoliths. The gods themselves are far beyond our reach or imagination.

Other movies flirt with the notion that good aliens are beyond us on the evolutionary scale and try to extrapolate from our knowledge of anthropology. From *Close Encounters of the Third Kind* to *The X-Files*, aliens are depicted as hairless creatures, with bulbous heads and efficient but unmuscled bodies. The assumption seems to be that we will evolve farther and farther away from our anthropoid origins. We will become hairless and have less use for our muscles. Our brains will expand and our eyes, our windows to the world, will become the dominant feature of our faces.

Still other good aliens are closer to noble realizations of human form. Their eminence often has roots in religion and myth. The visitor (David Bowie) in *The Man Who Fell to Earth* is explicitly a Christ figure. The emissary Klaatu is idealized in *The Day the Earth Stood Still* and suffers wounding, death, and resurrection.

Two movies of the 1980s flirted with the notion that our standards of beauty and perfection are parochial. *E. T. the Extra-Terrestrial* succeeded in making a scaly, reptilian creature lovable and admirable. And in *The Empire Strikes Back*, the character of Yoda showed that wisdom can come in small and glamorless packages. But if these aliens elude our common measures of beauty, their visceral appeal is hardly mysterious. E. T. has the warm, placating eyes of a small child or cuddly animal, while Yoda's features share the venerableness of those who have aged well and wisely.

If the good tend to be superhuman, bad aliens tend to be subhuman. If "human" in this context refers to domination over nature, extraterrestrials often threaten to reverse the process. They are nature run rampant. Shakespeare's Caliban, though an inhabitant of earth, is subhuman, alien to all that is humanly spiritual and a threat to the persons around him. Alternatively, bad aliens may be insects grown to horrific size, as in *Them!* or *Starship Troopers*. They may be reptilian or crustacean. The lobster-like creature in Georges Melies' *A Trip to the Moon* (1902), possibly the first movie with a claim to be called science fiction, is a distant ancestor of the carapaced beast in the *Alien* movies. Nature's threat may even come from the plant world. The various versions of *Invasion of the Body Snatchers* chronicle the success of alien pods in taking over the bodies and minds of humans. Invidious aliens may even be very primitive forms of life with unnatural powers of replication, simple-celled creatures threatening to squeeze us out *(The Blob)*.

This catalog of aliens is notable in two ways. All of the projects are movies. And virtually all dispense with the craft of the transformational makeup artist. Superhuman aliens are either unimaginable *(2001)* and therefore unimagined, or they are barely imaginable, seen only in fever dreams and in shadows *(Close Encounters, X-Files)*, or they are altogether human, but in a peculiarly unblemished form *(Man Who Fell to Earth)*. Both Yoda and E. T. were puppets and animatronic creations.

The same can be said about bad aliens. Large insects, reptiles, crustaceans, and amoebas are also produced through animatronics, simple enlargement coupled with sophisticated camerawork, and computer simulation. Reptilian aliens of forty years ago were men in rubber suits *(The Creature from the Black Lagoon)*, but such beasts are now (and were then) the stuff of self-parody.

We saw that the demands of movies and TV series diverge. The aliens in movies are often nonhuman and nonhumanoid, and the plot is not really about them at all. When the aliens are superhuman, the story typically involves their effect on human affairs. *2001, Star Wars, E. T.,* and *Close Encounters* are all about the response of human beings to unprecedented physical and moral challenges. With subhuman aliens, the story is elemental and also about persons, about their capacity to understand and escape dire threats. Stories of this kind are usually the stuff of a single episode, reaching a denouement in two hours or less.

TV series comprise not a single and simple trajectory of story but a collection of plots that intersect and echo the range of dramatic situations that persons fall into over time. For aliens to figure significantly in such experiences, they have to be nearly human in their understanding, motives, and behavior. As such, they can be the vehicle for metaphorical explorations of alienness, literally otherness, in the familiar world. This role opens up a world of possibility for the makeup artist who must render them as variations on humanity, variations designed to remind us of our possible selves and of all those others in our familiar world who are the elusive objects of our understanding and empathy.

Faces Only an Alien Mother Could Love

Science fiction television series have been interlopers on television. Other genres—police series, lawyer series, westerns, genteel mysteries, evening soap operas—have waxed and waned in popularity but have never lost their substantial presence and equally substantial following. They have generally taken the high road of network broadcast rather than the lower road of syndication.

Science fiction has never had more than a beachhead on network television. The main successes have come from the TV equivalent of outer space, not only syndication but also the cable stations. In hindsight, *Star Trek* is generally credited with repopulating the television world with aliens and spaceships. In its initial incarnation, *Star Trek* was a low-budget (network) enterprise, one that began with little visibility and less promise. Only toward the end of its original three-year run did the intensity of its impact and the staying power of its cult following become evident. Three spinoff series have followed, along with (to date) eight movies.

Star Trek did not revive futuristic science fiction. Such series were popular in the embryo years of television with such minibudget shows as *Captain Video*, *Buck Rogers*, and *Tom Corbett: Space Cadet*. All vanished as television "matured." And in the years after *Star Trek* became entrenched, an endless series of imitators bit the dust more quickly than villains in old-time westerns. The *Star Trek* formula, such as it is, has been paradoxically easy to replicate (in spinoffs) and impossible to imitate.

Two series that owe little to *Star Trek* have had their own cult followings. In both cases, as with *Star Trek*, the effect has been cumulative. It took at least three seasons of cultivation to produce a harvest of interest. *The X-Files* has in fact had as much of the spotlight as it could possibly want, risking overexposure. The series traffics on the fine line between the occult and the realm of aliens. Its aliens are siblings of the visitors in *Close Encounters*, the bug-eyed, unmuscled, large-craniumed, greenish-white creatures of generic science fiction cartoons. The business of *X-Files* is not with aliens but with government conspiracies and cover-ups and with the presence of occult forces beyond our understanding. Its obsessions are with the present and not the future, with reality and not metaphor.

By contrast, the other success, *Babylon 5*, more a critical than a popular success, is at first glance in the *Star Trek* mode. It takes us three centuries into the future, takes interplanetary travel for granted, and concerns the trafficking between humans and aliens at the time when other worlds are either friendly or hostile. The design of its starships and the "scientific" premises of its technologies are similar to those of *Star Trek*.

But *Babylon 5* had a special mission. While all of the *Star Trek* series have been open-ended, with each episode contemplating a new predicament, *Babylon 5* had a five-year plan. The story, ambitiously metaphorical, had a trajectory implicit from its inception. The configuration and interaction of parts had the kind of complexity and determinateness that early cosmologists and later historiographers have sought in human experience as a whole. The aliens and the realms they represent have many covert dimensions.

Babylon 5 stumbled early in the United States, threatened with cancellation after its third and fourth seasons. Its major and overwhelming success was outside the U.S., where it was regularly applauded as the "best science fiction series of all time." Be that as it may, it had a density and texture that warrant explication. And its aliens were the most richly conceived of all.

We shall explore *Babylon 5* in the next part of this chapter. But the aliens of *Star Trek* and some other series have also challenged the art of makeup. It was a foregone conclusion that, if the interactions between humans and aliens were to mirror the dilemmas of human life, aliens would have to be humanoid. *Star Trek* committed itself early to a technically inexpensive code of minimal alienness. Thus Dr. Spock, the Vulcan in the original series, had pointed ears and diagonal eyebrows, along with a preternaturally spiky hairdo. It is said that the ears presented makeup artist John Chambers with a significant challenge, but to the non-expert eye the makeup job is minimal. Dr. Spock looks suspiciously human and suspiciously like Leonard Nimoy, who portrays him. The tradition of minimalism persists in the permanent cast of aliens in *Star Trek: Deep Space Nine* and *Star Trek: Voyager*, who are distinguished in one case by furrows on the bridge of a nose and in another by hieratic tattoos above the left brow.

Over the years there has been a fairly close connection between the villainy and inhumanity of characters on *Star Trek* and the amount and thickness of the rubber on their faces. The makeup of the Jem Ha'dar, destructive to the core, is reptilian; it is thick enough to be distractingly masklike and to prevent the actors from expressing emotion at all. Such villains, one must suppose, are one-dimensional killing machines who have no need to express anything subtler than a command.

Some of the recurring and more individualized characters are also plagued with relatively inflexible makeups. Worf, one of the regular characters in *Star Trek: The Next Generation*, is Klingon, who are stern aliens feared for their aggressiveness and cunning intelligence. They are distinguished by bony, menacing foreheads and recessed hairlines. For the most part, these prosthetic appliances do not so much transform the actors' physiognomy from a human configuration as designate the characters' alienness as might a badge or symbol. And yet the Klingon foreheads, clearly used to convey sternness, also go along with a mask-like expressionlessness that draws attention to the artificiality of the makeup.

Bigger budgets, however, can produce or allow for better Klingons. In the movie *Star Trek VI: The Undiscovered Country*, the screenplay called for negotiations between humans and a distinguished war council of Klingon luminaries. The challenge for the production's makeup team, which included Rick Stratton and Richard Snell, was twofold: to make Klingons who were differentiable one from another, just as humans are, and to integrate prosthetic foreheads as parts of plausible, expressive faces. In Snell's exemplary work on Christopher Plum-

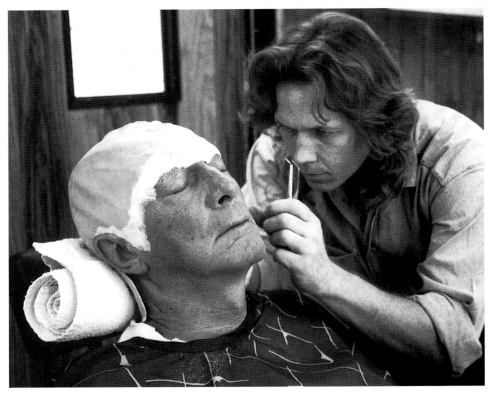

Figure 5.1. Richard Snell applies Christopher Plummer's makeup for *Star Trek VI: The Undiscovered Country*.

Figure 5.2.
Christopher Plummer
in full regalia
for *Star Trek VI.*

mer, facial rigidity gave way to an embodiment of authority, craft, and dignity. Subtle tricks, the suggestion for example of a metal eye patch bolted (with microscopically enscribed bolts) to an empty eyesocket, make us sense the bones beneath the skin.

Even when they serve up thick rubber faces, inescapably fake, *Star Trek*'s makeup artists indulge a commedia dell'arte style of wit and deliberate exaggeration. In the *Deep Space Nine* series, Quark and his kinsmen are Ferengi, a race of unscrupulous petit bourgeoisie who are the perfect (and perfectly ridiculous) embodiment of an utterly familiar economic ideal, the entrepreneur single-mindedly out to maximize his profits. Morals, esthetics, and emotions rarely get in their way. Their large ears are designed to hear every rumor, their conspicuous cranial lobes work overtime to process useful strategies, and their snaggleteeth

Figure 5.3. Armin Shimmerman

Figure 5.4. Shimmerman as Quark (*Star Trek: Deep Space Nine*). Makeup by Michael Westmore's team of artists.

let nothing escape. The Ferengi are like Shakespeare's clowns and commoners; we are invited to laugh at them more than with them. We can take neither their looks nor nature seriously. (And yet of course the market-based attitudes that animate them remain a serious economic model of optimal capitalist behavior.)

Another of the regulars on *Deep Space Nine* is, in a sense, a living metaphor for acting and the craft of makeup. Odo, as portrayed by Rene Auberjonois, is a shape-shifter. His appearance among humans, as a security officer on Deep Space Nine, has an unfinished quality—as if he were melting slightly or as if his transition from a viscous liquid to a solid state had been arrested. He can liquefy completely and assume an array of forms. Odo's one-piece prosthetic mask is ingenious. It commands assent: of course, a shape-shifter would appear unfinished in just this way. And as metaphor it reminds us that we ourselves are works in progress capable of shifting attitudes, if not shapes, from context to context, that actors deliberately shift shapes, and that the art of makeup addresses both our determinateness and our fantasies of change.

The ubiquitousness of *Star Trek* casts a shadow over other series with extraterrestrials. The series *Alien Nation* deserves mention. The story is set in the present. The series and the movie on which it is based presume that now, at the end of the twentieth century, we have been joined by a race of beings from space,

Newcomers. Their spaceship, containing hundreds of thousands of slaves dominated by an authoritarian higher caste, has been diverted to Earth. The Newcomers, with astonishing speed, have taken up positions in all walks of American life, in all professions, and at all levels of society. They have learned our language and customs and have assimilated.

The Newcomers differ from us in important ways. They are hairless, with large crania and patches in abstract patterns on their heads and backs. Their dietary habits (sour milk and beavers are special treats), religious practices, "erogenous zones," and methods of procreation (the male bears the child) all differ from our own. They are, if anything, superior to us, notable for their strength, olfactory and visual capacities, memory, and intelligence. The Newcomers we meet are for the most part moral exemplars—considerate, tolerant, empathetic. At the same time it is made clear that collectively they are as diverse as we are, harboring bigots and fanatics in the midst.

Can a metaphor be more transparent than this? The challenges of accepting and integrating the Newcomers, of according them civil rights, of intermarrying, and of configuring our standards of beauty, belief, and respect to embrace them are all echoes of our long-standing problems with race. Discrimination against

Figure 5.5. Rene Auberjonois

Figure 5.6. Auberjonois as the shape-shifter Odo. Makeup by Paramount makeup artists under Michael Westmore's supervision.

Figure 5.7. Eric Pierpoint

Figure 5.8. Pierpoint as George Francisco, the Newcomer police detective in *Alien Nation*. Makeup by Rick Stratton and Richard Snell.

Newcomers is portrayed as bigotry; their entitlement to equal treatment and equal rights is presumed. The premise that legal and social recognition should be based on personal qualities and not on one's history, race, ethnicity, or class background is always honored. And the personal qualities of the Newcomers make them more human than humans.

The makeup for the Newcomers is disarmingly simple. Actors wear a simple prosthetic piece that extends from just below the eyebrows back over the head down the lower part of the neck, covering the actor's ears. The piece is thick and padded to suggest a large cranial cavity. The surface is covered with brown patches in distinctive and varied patterns. The actor's eyes, nose, mouth, chin, and cheeks are uncovered, unencumbered.

Our sense of the Newcomers mirrors our response to a relatively unfamiliar race. It is hard to tell Newcomers apart, echoing the cliché that Westerners all look alike to Asians, and vice versa. But we learn the differences. We also have to modify our sense of beauty. What effect does hairlessness, earlessness, and a large head have on our sensibilities when it is not a deformity but the norm? The effect of the makeup on actors' appearances is also variable and surprising. Some are radically transformed, nearly unrecognizable. Others survive the transition with their familiarity intact.

The *Alien Nation* franchise survived for a couple of seasons, sputtering out in a series of TV movies. The *Star Trek* series, still flourishing, also gives strong hints of exhaustion of ideas. But the recent series with by far the most imaginative representation of aliens was *Babylon 5*.

Babylonians: An Introduction

Babylon 5, planned as a five-year television series taking its characters and human/universal history from 2257 to 2262, completed its initial self-ascribed mandate in 1998. It earned a cult following and major awards outside the United States, while struggling for recognition at home. It was unique among TV series in its epic scope. The trajectory of its plot was planned from the beginning. Unlike *Star Trek*, for example, it was for the most part not episodic, with each separate story self-contained. Nor did it simply incorporate story arcs bridging several episodes. The other rare TV series that built an entire series around an evolving story (*The Fugitive, The Prisoner* are examples) focused on the fate and mystery of one protagonist, not humanity.

Babylon 5 was the invention of J. Michael Straczynski, who wrote most of the scripts and guided every aspect of the show. Babylon 5 itself is an outpost in space, a free-trading, self-governing station that is home to a quarter million humans and aliens. Its main officers are human, and its main affiliation is initially with Earth Alliance, a collectivity of human and alien military and political forces that patrols much of the explored universe. After the government on Earth is subverted through a coup and the president is assassinated, Babylon 5 breaks free from Earth Alliance, leading the forces that seek the restoration of democratic values and practices.

The political and military situation of Babylon 5 and its home planet defines one plane on which the series operates, arguably the least interesting one. Even on this plane, however, the series poses intractable questions. A subclass of humans with telepathic powers are sought out, trained, and employed by the government as an intelligence agency, the Psi Corps. There are, of course, dissident telepaths, rogue telepaths, and private telepaths unknown to the government. *Babylon 5* regularly poses questions about what the role of telepaths in general society can be, whether the social and political power of telepaths can be contained, and whether open government can survive in such a context. (Telepaths pay a heavy psychological price for their talent.)

The humans on Babylon 5 work with and among countless aliens. Three groups seem most important in the evolving interplanetary situation in the mid-twenty-third century. Each is represented by an ambassador who is a key player in the politics of Babylon 5. The Minbari, with whom the humans had earlier fought a bitter war, are highly evolved technologically and spiritually. Time travel, austere formality, and a simple but rich esthetic are features of their civilization. Their cities are crystalline. Their society and government is a representative structure in which three castes—the religious, the military, and the workers—are balanced uneasily.

The Centauri cultivate a rococo style of life and politics. Their mandarinate squanders its abundant resources on self-indulgence and court intrigue. Their role among civilizations is characterized by imperial and colonial adventurism and opportunism. Their traditional enemies and foils are the Narn, reptilian in appearance and backward-looking in their culture and politics. They are a dark, humorless, and pessimistic race, whose religion and values are governed by occult texts that emphasize predestination and teach stoicism. Their history includes enslavement and near annihilation by the Centauri.

If dealing with the Minbari, the Centauri, and the Narn constitutes the second plane of *Babylon 5*, one of comparative civilizations and culture, the third plane of *Babylon 5* is less historical or political and more metaphysical. Major players in the fate of mankind are beings that are barely accessible to us, given our parameters of space and time. Some (the First Ones) assume recognizable quasi-human physical form but make it clear that they existed before the advent of all known civilizations. They stand outside evolution, or life and death, and they have godlike powers to affect what we do and to foresee what will happen.

If the First Ones are benign, other barely accessible beings are not. The Shadows are a malign force, never quite incarnated, that have technologies beyond our comprehension but that generally work through their influence on species that occupy time and space. They can be repelled and detected through intelligible strategies but their true nature and identity remain obscure. Like the First Ones, they belong simultaneously to the infinite past and future.

The Vorlons are a more stable and abiding presence. They are represented by an ambassador on Babylon 5, but he lives within his own "encounter suit," a protective environment that sustains him and shields his identity. The Vorlons are marginally within the time and space constraints of humans, Minbari, etc. Like the First Ones, they are clairvoyant; like the Shadows, they employ an "organic" technology whereby their environment, for example their space vehicles, are extensions of their living being, capable of life and vulnerable to death. Deprived of their encounter suits, they do not assume a stable physical presence in human (or other) eyes. Their appearance is in the eye of the beholder, who sees them in the perfected image of his or her own civilization.

The three planes of *Babylon 5*—the struggle between Earth and Babylon 5, the interplay of civilizations and cultures, the metaphysics of predestination and wars outside space and time—coexist in a story of intimidating complexity. As a cult phenomenon, the *faux* history of each character and each culture within Babylon 5 is subject to infinite elaboration and refinement. But our main focus is not the story but the aliens. How are they visualized and realized? What makes them distinctive?

The aliens of *Babylon 5* tote heavy symbolic baggage. Just as the villains and ingenues in oldtime melodramas had a distinctive look, the aliens must have an appearance that fits the dispositions of their civilization. It must also be variable, so that the Minbari, Narn, and Centauri are distinguishable as individuals. And it must be convincing, to the point that we are not reminded at every turn that these are actors wearing rubber prosthetics. The makeup must take over, so that we see the aliens in terms of a distinctive look and facial structure, a characteristic physiognomy crafted by nature and evolution and not the makeup technician. And it helps if there is a hint of humor, a sense that the characters mock human foibles and can be seen as an incarnated hyperbolic version of human tendencies.

The Faces of Babylon 5

The work of John Vulich and his staff at Optic Nerve achieves all of these aims. Although Vulich did not work on the pilot TV film for the series and inherited some designs, most of the aliens on *Babylon 5* are the product of his fertile imagination. The alien makeups come in three types. The faces of the Minbari and the Centauri, several of whom are important and ubiquitous players on Babylon 5, must be fully expressive, and the makeup, while distinctive, must allow individuals to be recognized easily. Other alien species—for example, the Narn, the Drazi, and the Markab—share fewer features with humans and, more often than not, are background figures. Their appearance is more generic. Aliens in a third category, while no doubt representative of

Figure 5.9. Peter Jurasik

their kind, are unique characters within the confines of *Babylon 5*. These characters show Vulich's imagination at full throttle. They involve complete transformations of the actor, are utterly convincing as alternative physiognomies, and correlate with the nature and spirit of the character.

Londo Mollari (played by Peter Jurasik) is the Centauri ambassador to Babylon 5, eventually destined to be prime minister in the Centauri government. The Centauri civilization mirrors the royal courts of prerevolutionary Europe in the seventeenth and eighteenth centuries. Society is hierarchic, militaristic, and authoritarian; the esthetic is baroque to rococo; and intrigue and duplicity keep the wheels of government spinning. Londo is the perfect specimen of his kind. He is vain enough to have and express disdain for others, but shrewd enough not to underestimate them, and to anticipate setbacks and shape events to his own ends. Self-pampering, self-pitying, and overfed, he is nonetheless a survivor. His appearance fits; his soft features belie his quick, darting, all-seeing, all-knowing eyes. Like all Centauri, his broad forehead ends in a sweeping crown of sharp quills, as ostentatious as the elaborate powder wigs of eighteenth-century nobles.

The makeup for the Minbari, like that of the Centauri, reconfigures the actor's forehead and hair leaving the lower face uncovered and mobile. The Minbari civilization is as austere and plain as the Centauri's is self-indulgent and ornate. The buildings of the Minbari are crystal palaces. Insubstantial light and shadow take the place of concrete objects in their environments. They are strictly disciplined, individually and collectively. Their pale, finely etched features are topped with a high-domed forehead, faintly mottled in blue, and an external

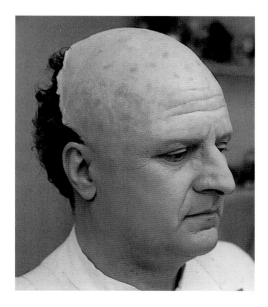

Figures 5.10, 5.11. Jurasik becomes the crafty and subtle Londo Mollari in *Babylon 5*. Makeup by John Vulich/Optic Nerve.

bone embraces and anchors the back of their heads and necks. Their brows are severely arched, and their look is one of skeptical intelligence.

The Minbari ambassador, Delenn, played by Mira Furlan, becomes one of the most influential players in the politics of Babylon 5 as well as the lover of the head of the station, Commander John Sheridan. In the first season of *Babylon 5*, Delenn's appearance is that of all Minbari. Partly for political and spiritual reasons she later undergoes a metamorphosis, becoming half-human in appearance and demeanor. Her arched brows and a vestigial bone cradling her hair remain her only Minbari features.

Delenn is not the only figure to cross the permeable barrier between humans and Minbari. Sheridan's predecessor as commander of Babylon 5, Jeffrey Sinclair (played by Michael O'Hare), undergoes the opposite transformation, reverting to his identity as Valen, a Minbari founder and prophet. The modification of O'Hare's appearance is subtle.

In configuring the Narns, John Vulich is in something of a bind. The Narns look like a cross between an alligator and a human. The makeup fully covers and transforms the actor, giving him or her deepset red eyes, sunken cheeks, a pointed chin, and a scaly leathery skin. The problem is that it is hard to tell Narns apart. One face may be wider, another more furrowed—but in the absence of acute scrutiny one Narn looks like another, just as alligators, turtles, and frogs do.

Figure 5.12. Mira Furlan

Figures 5.13, 5.14. Delenn, the Minbari ambassador played by Mira Furlan on *Babylon 5*, morphs in the second season into an alien-human hybrid.

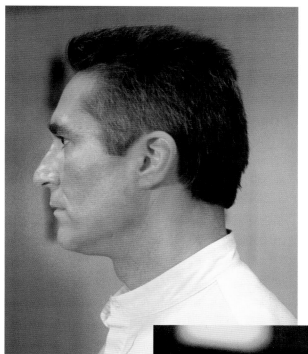

Figure 5.15. Michael O'Hare

Figure 5.16. O'Hare, as Jeffrey Sinclair on *Babylon 5*, also assumes his second identity as the venerable Minbari elder, Valen. Makeup by John Vulich/Optic Nerve.

Nonetheless, the Narn makeup effectively conveys the nature of Narns as a primitive people, beseiged and enslaved both by its darkly mystical beliefs and by the oppression of its enemies. They look only recently evolved from creatures that might slither in caves. A smile on the face of a Narn is unsettling.

Even more than the Narn, the Drazi—a simple-minded, childlike, but belligerent species—are barely differentiable. They are as much insectoid as reptilian. Their faces are more like carapaces, made of shingled embossed scales, and they are singularly expressionless. If there is no need to differentiate among Drazi because they present themselves as an unindividuated swarm, the same cannot be said of the Markab people. The Markabs, a race that is eventually extinguished by a viral epidemic, is a highly differentiated people, achieving levels of intelligence and education similar to humans. They have doctors and scientists. The characteristic Markab visage is noseless with a hairless, bulbous cranium adorned in a pattern of circular grooves.

Initially the Markabs were created en masse with slip-on masks. When this inhibited their facial expression and made them hard to distinguish, Vulich's team used a more individualized strategy for the main Markab characters. Using the same technique as for some of the Drazi, Narns, and others, Vulich created a two- or three-piece set of foam prosthetics. The main piece is a cowl that covers the head and neck to the shoulders and midchest, leaving only the front of the face

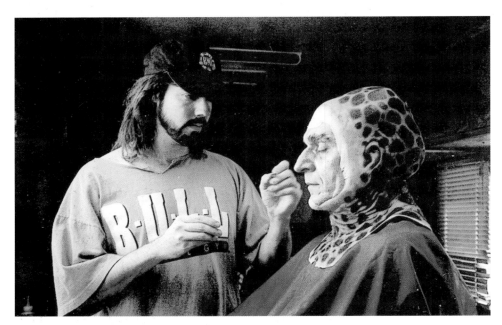

Figure 5.17. Andreas Katsulis becomes, in the hands of Will Huff, the powerful, complex Narn ambassador, G'Kar. Makeup by John Vulich/Optic Nerve.

Figures 5.18, 5.19. Two views of G'Kar. Makeup by John Vulich/Optic Nerve.

Figure 5.20. Kim Strauss

Figures 5.21, 5.22 (this page), **5.23, 5.24** (opposite page). At the hands of *Babylon 5*'s Optic Nerve makeup artists, Kim Strauss becomes, respectively, a Drazi (shown with Will Huff), the Markab ambassador, a Narn, and a character in *B5*'s sister series, *Hypernauts*.

Figure 5.25. Michael McKenzie

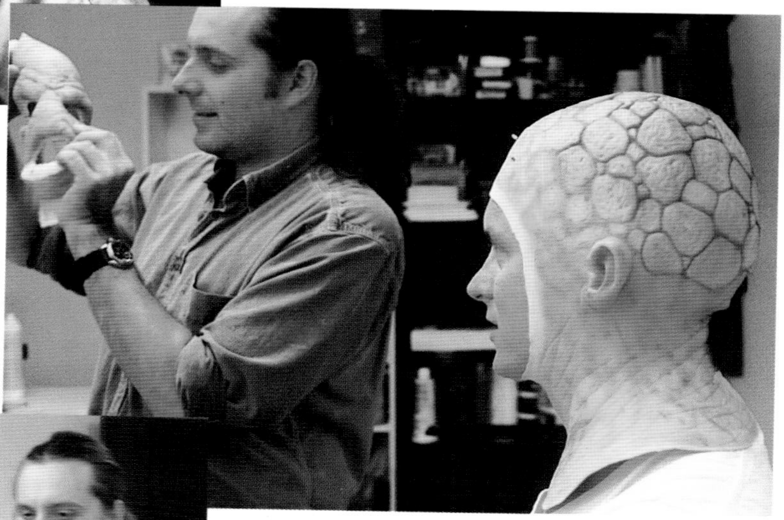

Figures 5.26, 5.27, 5.28 (opposite top).
Transformed by John Vulich, McKenzie becomes
a Markab victim. Makeup by Optic Nerve.

Figure 5.29. Another face of
Michael McKenzie, as an
alien assassin on *Babylon 5*.
Makeup by John Vulich/
Optic Nerve.

Figure 5.30. Wayne Alexander

bare. The face, in turn, is completely covered with a delicately sculpted thin appliance that, while fully transforming the actor, allows for effective expression.

John Vulich's flair for devising "real" aliens is most evident in characters that stand as unique. The cowl-and-mask approach at its most effective was used for Lorien (played by Wayne Alexander), the most venerable of the First Ones. The idea behind such characters as Lorien is one that has often animated religion and cosmology, that the universe instantiates an intelligence that comprehends and sustains it. The First Ones are anterior to space and time and have "seen it all," witnessed all of cosmological and human history—and know the future. They intervene by direct action, incarnate, only at critical moments.

Visualizing Lorien is a unique problem. The character must convey infinite age, limitless wisdom, and an incarnation of justice and benevolence. (And of course the makeup must not look like a rubber mask.) The remarkably effective design recapitulates the Renaissance view of the wise men who attended God's representative on earth.

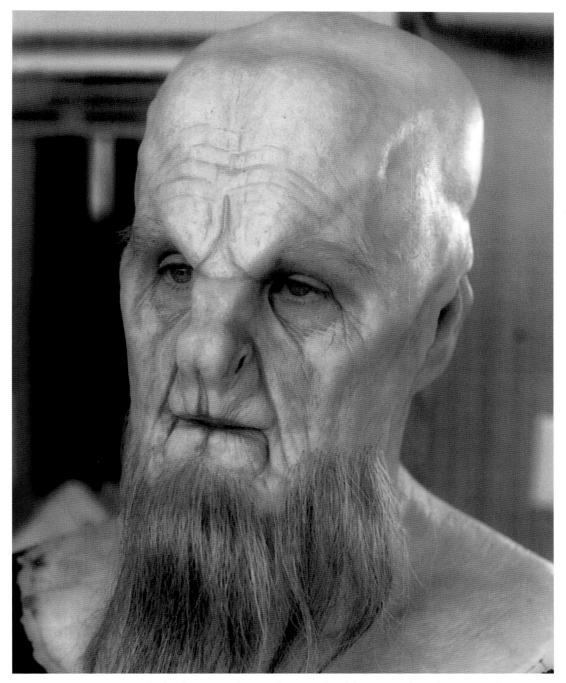

Figure 5.31. Lorien, the first being (yes, the very first!), as played by Wayne Alexander. Makeup by John Vulich/Optic Nerve.

Venerable in a less exalted way is The Muta'do (played by Soon-Tek Oh). In a first-season episode, "T.K.O.," the character is the referee at an inter-alien martial arts competition, functioning as judge and keeper of order. Again, the artists at Optic Nerve use a cowl-and-mask with a facial design that conveys dignity and authority. The makeup delivers a double punch. The first effect is one of estrangement, even horror, at the deeply furrowed skin, slit nose, and bumpy cranium. But one quickly comes to take the character on his own serious terms.

Still more mundane, venting sardonic wit at his station in life, is Zathras, a

Figure 5.32. Soon-Tek Oh

Figure 5.33. Oh as the referee in the *Babylon 5* episode "T.K.O." Makeup by John Vulich/Optic Nerve.

time-traveling jack-of-all-trades, aged and ageless, indispensable aide-de-camp of Sinclair/Valen (the erstwhile commander of Babylon 5, translated into Minbari prophet). Zathras, played by Tim Choate, appears in a few episodes, dependably stealing the spotlight. He claims to be one of ten identical siblings, all (necessarily) named Zathras. He is wily and whiny to a fault, the ultimate unappreciated facilitator with the look of a sleek and clever rodent. The prosthetics and wig, along with Zathras' accent and demeanor, so transformed Choate that fellow actors, seeing him for the first time out of makeup, dismissed his claim that he was in fact Zathras.

Figure 5.34. Tim Choate

Figure 5.35. Will Huff turns Tim Choate into Zathras.

Figure 5.36. Zathras, the comically inspired time-traveler in *Babylon 5*, is played by Tim Choate. Makeup by John Vulich/Optic Nerve

Figure 5.37. Eric Zivot

Figure 5.38. Spragg, a compatriot of Zathras, is incarnated by Eric Zivot. Makeup by John Vulich/Optic Nerve.

In one scene, Zathras confers with Spragg, a member of his own race. Wearing prosthetic pieces originally modeled for Choate, the actor Eric Zivot is also convincingly transformed. More than any other characters in *Babylon 5*, Zathras and his tribe are the twenty-third century's equivalent of Shakespeare's comic foils, his wise fools.

Kosh, the Vorlon ambassador to Babylon 5, generally appears in a portable, self-contained encounter suit, from which he broadcasts words and flashes of light. His appearance remains a mystery and subject of speculation. Only when John Sheridan, the commander of Babylon 5, is endangered by an explosion on a monorail and plunges to certain death do we see more of Kosh and glimpse the nature of Vorlons. An angelic figure, shrouded in light, flies up from the encounter suit to rescue Sheridan and ease him to the ground. But various observers, human and alien, each see the angelic figure as an idealization of its own race. Is it the nature of Vorlons to be idealized creatures of light, or (as the characters' ruminations imply) have we been programmed to perceive Vorlons in this way?

The makeup for Josh Patton, the actor who played the human and Minbari incarnations of Kosh, consists of thin prosthetic appliances that smooth out and accentuate his features. The effect of an angelic ideal is realized, and the change is as thorough as it is simple. Wearing equally effective makeup, Walter Phelan embodies the Narn and Drazi versions of the idealized Kosh.

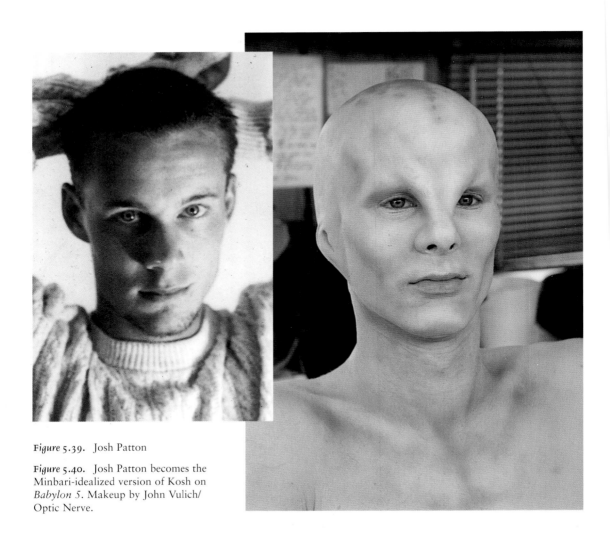

Figure 5.39. Josh Patton

Figure 5.40. Josh Patton becomes the Minbari-idealized version of Kosh on *Babylon 5*. Makeup by John Vulich/Optic Nerve.

Figure 5.41. For contrast, here is Josh Patton in a more demonic mode for *Tales from the Crypt* (see also Figures 4.6, 4.7). Makeup by Todd Masters; applied by James Rohland.

Figure 5.42 (below left). Walter Phelan

Figures 5.43 (below right), 5.44 (next page). Phelan appears as the idealized Narn and idealized Drazi versions of Kosh on *Babylon 5*. Makeup by John Vulich/Optic Nerve.

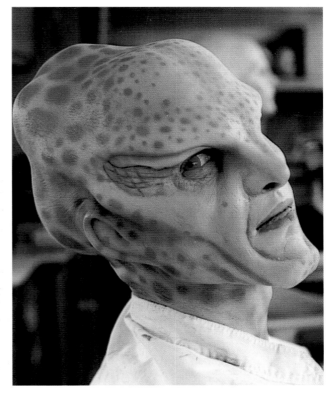

Some of John Vulich's favorite unique aliens come to life through wildly expressive masks that redistribute eyes, mouths, and ears without regard to function. Although they can only be "background aliens," these characters reflect the wide ambit of Babylon 5. In their wit and strangeness, they are the distant cousins of Rick Baker's breakthrough makeups for the barroom scene in *Star Wars*.

The aliens of *Babylon 5* ask to be taken seriously as beings with a distinctive inner and outer life. Optic Nerve's makeup invites us to see them not as persons-behind-rubber but as characters with their own evolutionary history, their own physicality, their own standards of beauty and homeliness, their own history, vices, and virtues. This frees the actor beneath—just as it frees us to take them as metaphors for everyday otherness in all its possibilities.

Figures 5.45, 5.46, 5.47, 5.48, 5.49, 5.50. The range of aliens on *Babylon 5* is endless. Makeup by John Vulich/Optic Nerve.

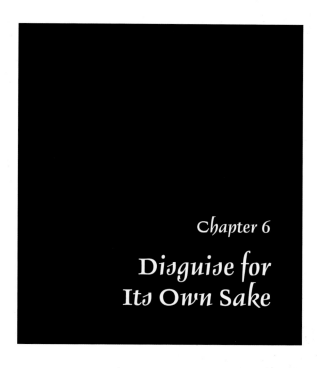

Chapter 6

Disguise for Its Own Sake

There will be time, there will be time
To prepare a face to meet the faces that you meet.
T. S. Eliot, "The Love Song of J. Alfred Prufrock"

In months, not years, the mask becomes the face.
Mignon McLaughlin, *The Second Neurotic's Notebook*

Occasions for Disguise

Consider the advantages of invisibility. You can do mischief—more than mischief, real harm—and avoid responsibility. If others cannot see you acting, they cannot identify you. Not only harm doing is at issue, of course. You can do good without having to be smothered with praise. You can be foolish without incurring others' disrespect. You can be inconsistent without facing argument and censure.

And yet, being invisible is often not a comfortable fantasy. In stories it is a predicament, a state of desperation in which one cannot get the expected attention of others, a state in which friends and lovers go about their lives as if one were dead. Perhaps luckily, with all its advantages and disadvantages, invisibility is still beyond our reach.

But the functional equivalent of invisibility is at hand. Fantasies about disguise go back as far as fantasies about being invisible. In many fantasies about disguise, the end matters less than the means; it is less important who one becomes than that one ceases to be oneself. Disguise, thus, is invisibility on the cheap. One ceases to be recognizable and suspends personal responsibility without the difficulty and drawbacks of being incorporeal.

Like invisibility, disguise is a two-edged sword. Its advantage is that it confers special powers. Figuratively, or even literally, it lets one get away with murder. Fantasies and thoughts of invisibility make us aware of the fragility of law, order, and civilization, aware of how much social peace depends on being able to recognize others and hold them responsible.

The disadvantages are also immediate and disturbing. Disguise is the opposite of amnesia. With amnesia one retains one's outward appearance, one's recognizability by others, but loses the subjective continuity of life through memory. To be disguised, on the other hand, is to be known only to oneself. Interpersonal ties are on hiatus. Do we depend on recognition for our sense of who we are? Does a breakdown threaten our sense of identity? The dark side of disguise is not only objective but subjective. Not only does it allow us to threaten and harm others, but it undercuts social patterns and expectations that enable us to recognize ourselves.

If the technology of becoming invisible is unavailable, what about the technology of disguise? The question is ambiguous, and the answer depends on the disguiser's purpose. One simple purpose is to avoid recognition. Terrorists, revolutionaries, criminals, and police all know that a simple ski mask suffices. A more complex purpose is to be unrecognizable without looking masked. This purpose can be achieved variously. The most modest way is a straightforward alteration: dyeing hair, changing facial hair, creating a fake scar. At the other end of the range is the complete and convincing creation of a physiognomy altogether unlike the (literally) underlying subject, with the artifice totally concealed.

Makeup artists tend to think that it is barely possible to achieve disguise in this latter sense. The most important variable is the kind of scrutiny and attention that the disguise will undergo. A false face will pass muster if looked at briefly without suspicion in a context that does not put the observer on guard. But close observation of facial movements and expressions under varying conditions of light may well risk exposure. We saw in Chapter 3 that it is devilishly hard to make prosthetic materials move, stretch, and fold like skin, and hard as well to make them reflect light as does translucent and layered skin. Thus, achieving the perfect disguise is the Mount Everest (or one of the Everests) of the art of makeup.

But what cannot be done in life can often be done in the movies. Awkward movements and revealing lighting are eliminable in moviemaking. Even there, however, creating a convincing radical disguise is a challenge. Makeup artists come closest to playing God, by their own admission, when they must create a person who is totally new, who carries over no features and traits of the underlying model, and who is at the same time utterly, convincingly real. The injunction is pure, generic, and sweeping, not merely "Create an alien, or create a demon," but "Create a new being."

This test arises in three contexts. The first is obvious, stories about disguise. If the account in Chapter 2 is correct, fantasies about transforming ourselves have always been ubiquitous, tied intimately to our awareness of individuality and reflections about identity. Stories we have retold and cherished—in myths, fairy tales, legends, and plays—deal obsessively with disguise and metamorphosis.

In fact, what needs to be explained is the marginalization of these ideas in modern storytelling. The occasions in which contemporary movies, plays, and television exploit themes of disguise and physical change are rare. The skill that makeup artists use for these occasional challenges too often stays dormant.

The other two contexts in which makeup artists achieve disguise for its own sake have nothing to do with the inherent demands of stories and everything to do with the impatience of actors and makeup artists to show off their skill in creating new persons, whether stories invite them to do so or not. *Coming to America* and *The Nutty Professor* are dazzling collaborations between Eddie Murphy and the makeup artist Rick Baker. In each, Murphy plays multiple roles, unrecognizable in most of them. In principle, each role might have been played by a different actor with no change in the story; disguise is not part of the plot. But principle has nothing to do with the point of the enterprise, which is both to trick the audience and to let the audience in on the trick, and to accomplish this paradoxical purpose in a way that expands our appreciation of the possibilities of acting as metamorphosis.

A third context in which disguise is an end in itself is the simplest of all. Unlike other contexts, it has nothing to do with specific movie projects. Makeup artists often stretch their virtuosity to build a portfolio with private projects. They invent opportunities to demonstrate how far they can go with radical and convincing metamorphoses. These opportunities may have nothing to do with particular movie projects, television shows, or ads, and they are governed and limited only by the unfettered imagination and skills of the makeup artist.

Stories of Non-barefaced Deception

Without deceit, the world would be a poorer place. Or at least the world of the imagination, the world of the storyteller, would be poorer. Critics like to claim that there are only *n* many basic plots. Even if enumerating and distinguishing basic plots is an idle exercise, theorists are bound to acknowledge that deception plots are among the essential imaginative ploys.

We can deceive others in three ways: by what we say, by what we do, and by how we appear. Deception by appearance is of special interest in part because it seems to be passive. We all judge by appearances all the time. Deception by disguise exploits that necessity without using *explicit* lies. In that sense it seems uniquely to involve the complicity of the victim.

Our earliest storytellers were especially fascinated by disguise. A favorite trick of the gods in ancient myths is to assume disguises. In fact, it is impossible for the gods to appear as *themselves* to humans. They have necessarily to assume one temporary guise or another. But then, if they have no natural physical form, what sense are we to make of the idea of disguise? The answer, perhaps, lies in the intention behind their temporary appearance and the way in which it manifests itself. If the appearance gives evidence of their deity and is not intended to mislead, it is hardly a disguise.

In Greek mythology, intercourse and procreation between gods and humans face few biological obstacles. They are more the rule than the exception. We encounter lesser gods who count humans among their ancestors, as well as heroes who carry the genes of gods. The corporeal status of such beings is often unclear. While they are given physical descriptions and seem to have a fixed physical identity, they can change their form with apparent ease. Of special interest is Proteus, variously described as the son and attendant of Poseidon, as a god of water, and as a "prophet who dwells in the sea." Proteus had the power to grant magical requests but would only do so under coercion. "You must compel him by force. If you seize him and chain him, he will answer your questions in order to get released. . . . [W]hen he finds himself captured, his resort is to a power he possesses of changing himself into various forms. He will become a wild boar or a fierce tiger, a scaly dragon or lion with yellow mane. Or he will make a noise like the crackling of flames or the rush of water, so as to tempt you to let go the chain. . . . But you have only to keep him fast bound, and at last when he finds his arts unavailing, he will return to his own figure and obey your commands." Although the link is not explicitly made, one wonders how Proteus' association with water facilitates the fluidity of his change of form. (Other gods of water apparently lack his special talents.)

Perhaps the most familiar case of a mere mortal assuming disguise in the stories of ancient Greece is Odysseus' return to Ithaca. Cautious of his reception and uncertain whether his wife Penelope has been faithful, Odysseus mingles with the crowd of suitors until, satisfied that his doubts are groundless, he reveals his identity. The trick is made easier by the fact that his return is unexpected.

Myths in some other cultures force us to distinguish even more clearly between assuming a form and adopting a disguise. In Hindu mythology, Vishnu, the second in the triad of Hindu gods, is said to descend to earth in numerous incarnations (avatars), of which ten are significantly specified. The ninth, the most important, is in human form and is known as Krishna, an unconquerable warrior; the others are represented by such creatures as The Tortoise and The Fish. These incarnations of gods are not disguises, not generally intended to deceive by replacing a true form with a false one. Rather they are the characteristic way in which the gods make themselves accessible, ways in which they symbolize ideas and abstractions relevant to the human condition.

If Hindu mythology is best understood in intellectual and symbolic terms, with gods rarely manifesting the lesser human qualities of playfulness and trickery, Norse mythology stands in vivid contrast. Artifice and evil, often distinguished by quicksilver changes of form and appearance, dominate many stories in the Norse anthology. Loki, a giant who intrudes himself upon the gods and creates predicaments of danger, assumes various appearances, almost always with a malign motive and a pure intention to deceive.

When disguise plays a role in the transactions of Greek or Norse gods, the mechanism of disguise gets short shrift. The gods have the power to transubstantiate without resorting to cosmetics, masks, or wigs. A snap of the fingers or other trigger for magic will do fine. Mortals must not understand or underestimate the gods' powers.

Magical powers of disguise are also common in fairy tales. Like myths, fairy tales evolve over the history of a culture, often as part of an oral tradition. They often antedate individual authorship. The brothers Grimm, Hans Christian Andersen, and their counterparts are thought of more as compilers and amanuenses than as authors of tales. Unlike mythology, fairy tales do not describe a cosmology and a pantheon, nor do they embody the supernatural pseudohistory of a civilization. They are often cautionary tales addressed to children. Almost always they work by seducing children into identifying with the characters.

Transformations, when they occur, are magical. Disguise is effortless, and disguise is only one of the occasions for transformations. Persons may fall under a curse and be changed into toads or ravens. The kiss of a princess may be enough to turn the toad back into a prince. Rats may turn into coach horses at the touch of a fairy godmother's wand, and the enchantment may wear off simply because midnight has struck. With disarming ease, a wolf may assume the appearance of a grandmother. The transformation may be perfect or imperfect; the wolf's canines may threaten to give him away.

Fairy tale transformations are easy, psychologists remind us, because they reflect the point of view of children. For a child who cannot reconcile her loving mother with her mother-as-angry-disciplinarian, it is more natural to assume that mother has been transformed into a wolf or tiger ("not really mother at all") than to be reconciled to the inconstancy of human nature. In the same way, the child has no trouble transforming her blanket into an understanding companion or her teddy bear into a wise counselor. For children, wishes have transformative power, and the transformations can readily be carried out and readily be undone.

When we lose the magical thinking of fairy tales, we fall into the opposite assumption, that the physical, mental, and emotional equipment of a person is more or less invariant for life. We take for granted that the power to change is largely a postulate of magical and childish thinking. In Chapter 2, we asked whether that was simplistic. Physically, mentally, emotionally the extent to which we remain "the same person," the extent we are protean through circumstances or choice, is a dauntingly complicated problem. If our bodies look different to different persons, look different to ourselves at different times and in different moods, and in fact *do* take on different characteristics over time, then the mercurial metamorphoses of fairy tales may be a complex metaphor for something true. If one body can be host to multiple personalities, or to a personality that seems different to different persons, or to one that mellows or toughens over time, fairy tale thinking again captures psychological truth. Perhaps all princes turn into frogs (in the eyes of their princesses) some of the time, and all grandmothers harbor an inner wolf.

Growing up is not a matter of denying all metamorphoses and giving up fantasy, but of looking at experience critically. We may disagree about exactly where the frontier between reality and fantasy should be drawn (we may or may not be skeptical about extrasensory powers, about multiple personality claims), but we have generally shared criteria for seeing fairy tale switches as *literally* impossible, as calling for symbolic and not realistic interpretation. And when we turn back to mythology, which unlike fairy tales is tailored to fit the adult imagination, we accept that humans are denied the special powers that the gods take for granted.

Players: Faces and Roles

Our oldest storytelling traditions, myths and fairy tales, are matters not only of narration but of *acting out*. The penchant of the Greek gods for assuming and abandoning human guise at will was effected in Greek plays through the use of masks. Scholars disagree about how widely masks were used in Greek theater, but it is clear that they had a significant place in most premodern theatrical traditions.

It is sometimes hard to realize that realism is a late convention in the history of theater. We now take for granted that in most plays and movies characters will look and act like "real" persons and will not "unnaturally" change their appearance in the course of a play or movie. That is equally true whether the work is by Tennessee Williams, Neil Simon, or Stephen Spielberg. When we look back on premodern theater, the Greek anthology or the Japanese tradition of No plays, we tend to see them from our perspective as stylized and symbolic, as deviants from the constraint of realism.

But for most of theater's history the artifice of the stage was taken for granted, and the rules of ordinary off-stage experience were suspended. Actors, by putting on masks, could assume different personae, disguise themselves, and, if necessary, perpetrate deception with an ease and fluidity that satisfied the demands of the story. By shared convention this had nothing to do with the genuine morphic powers of real persons. Theater was one domain, real life another.

Because actors, like the gods of myth, did not so much wear their own natural faces but adopted faces for the sake of the play and the role (as in mythology, for the sake of communicating with a human audience), masks were not simply or primarily a vehicle for disguise. They were a way in which a character assumed a form and an appearance. The fact that they facilitated disguise was just a consequence of the technique and one of the ways in which technique came to influence plot. Even when masks had long ceased to be widely used, the convention that effective disguises could be assumed with the ease of a mask was followed in Elizabethan and Jacobean drama. Shakespeare used the convention shamelessly in such comedies as *Twelfth Night* and *The Merchant of Venice*.

In limited contexts, actors still sometimes use stylized masks *or* play multiple roles without effectively altering their appearance. Almost always, this happens on the stage and not in movies. Theater necessarily functions through conventions that defy realism. Rooms on stage lack a fourth wall; the acts of a play have their own artificial order and shape; the movements and blocking of the actors are dictated by the configuration of the theater; the actors' articulation is determined by the need to be heard throughout the auditorium, and so on. The artificiality of a narrator addressing the audience, of a stylized set, or of an actor playing multiple roles is one of many accepted conventions in a form that cannot exist without them.

Movies, on the other hand, convey the illusion of reality, that the camera (and the audience) is an interloper on a natural event in a real setting. Almost every movie aspires to a documentary *feel*. Acting styles, sets and lighting, and especially special effects in all their diversity and complexity are designed to do just one thing, achieve a sense of reality—that the villain is really beheaded, that Los Angeles is really buried in volcanic ash, that the Red Sea is really parting.

Movie-based expectations have, it seems, affected our attitudes toward theater. We are more resistant to its artificiality, its conventions. Plays have, for the most part, evolved to be more realistic and reliant on special effects, more like movies, and our leading playwrights are comfortable writing screenplays as well.

In this light, we come to identify actors with their faces, and we look at movie faces with realistic expectations. As a result, we look with skepticism at metamorphoses that we accepted in fairy tales, that we acknowledged in myth, and that we guardedly accepted on the stage. Our movie-grounded realism tells us that persons, characters and actors alike, cannot change their faces easily and convincingly. Certainly they cannot do so on whim, but only for a good reason. And when there is a compelling reason for a disguise, it requires very special talents and materials.

Thus, the occasion for disguise comes up rarely in recent and contemporary movies and plays. Note that our critical impulses respond in different ways to different kinds of special effects. We know that it is possible to blow up skyscrapers and behead soldiers or terrorists. So, even when we know that the events are only simulated, we accept the image of these events when they seem indistinguishable from reality. We also think we know what wars among galaxies and between alien armadas would look like, and we trust special effects wizards to satisfy our senses. But the challenge of disguise is different, and in a sense harder. We know perfectly well what it would be like to encounter someone who is perfectly disguised, whose rubber face gives nothing away and seems like flesh. *And* we know that *both in reality and in the movies* the effect is extraordinarily hard to achieve. Thus, the stakes for this particular kind of special effect are in some ways higher than for other effects and the available relatively low-tech methods of makeup artists are particularly challenged.

The movies in which convincing disguises play an effective role are therefore rare. And the criteria for what is acceptable have, as with all special effects, been rising constantly. Within the current conventions of movie realism, disguise as thorough and convincing transformation can be part of the story only when the character has both the motivation and the means to bring off a state-of-the-art prosthetic makeup.

With other kinds of effects, we are not committed to believing that the characters within the story use the same techniques as the effects artists who create the movie. The characters may blow up buildings, but the effects artists, as we know, are only exploding miniatures or using computer-generated illusions. The characters may engage in transgalactic battles in space, but we are pretty sure the effects artists are thoroughly earthbound. But with makeup effects the distinction between the character's tools and the effects artist's means collapses: the character in disguise is thought to use the same resources and techniques as the makeup effects artist. The disguise is in this sense real, and not, as with other effects, an illusion at all.

Consider how rarely a contemporary plot will demand that a character have the motivation and means to do a full-blown transformational makeup. A criminal wanting anonymity will usually need only a ski mask or stocking. If she needs a disguise without drawing unwanted attention to herself, then a wig or dark glasses will work. Similarly, an undercover cop would be foolish to infiltrate groups that are likely to recognize her and equally foolish to wear a false face that may look inauthentic or need repair. The camouflage will simply consist of the right clothes and attitude.

It is no wonder, then, that few plots of movies or television dramas require disguises that are full transformational makeups, that makeup artists rarely have the chance to show off this kind of magic. If, in fact, it would be mad for most characters to believe that they could disguise themselves effectively, then the characters who attempt this are likely to be mad. And if the challenge of disguise is, in a realistic setting, almost insuperable, then the projects that involve it will flirt with constraints of realism, will involve the kinds of stories, like Shakespeare's, that ask us to suspend disbelief.

Taking Disguise Seriously

Let's assume that the modern era of prosthetic appliances that have a chance of withstanding close scrutiny begins, in the 1950s, with the generation that includes such artists as Dick Smith and John Chambers. John Huston's *The List of Adrian Messenger* (1963) celebrates the perverse talent of its homicidal protagonist to assume almost any appearance. Implicitly it celebrates John Chambers' facility at manipulating the appearance of Kirk Douglas, in the role of a distant heir to the Scottish estate of Gleneyre, so that he shows up to commit murder in five faces other than his own.

Huston's movie is an adaptation of a Philip MacDonald novel, but Huston is intoxicated by the possibilities and implications of disguise in ways that MacDonald never considered. Not only does Douglas wear prosthetic faces that turn him into an elderly country parson and a scurvy wharf rat, but other famous actors (Frank Sinatra, Burt Lancaster, Robert Mitchum, and Tony Curtis) all show up in bit parts wearing disguises. Huston's playfulness with the element of disguise goes far beyond the demands of the plot, and even seems to subvert it.

Sinatra and company never appear in their own faces (at least not before they line up for a coda in which they simply strip away their masks), and the fact that they are disguised plays no part in the plot. Moreover, the fact that the Douglas character *is* disguised is revealed early in an elaborate scene in which, with surgical precision, he removes his fake contact lens, his teeth, his wig and bald cap, and finally his rubber face. From that point on, his impostures may fool the other characters, but not the audience. And much of the mystery is, it seems, flushed away along with his prosthetic face. Huston thus indulges the finesse of disguise at the cost of his story, and the movie becomes a whydunnit rather than a whodunnit.

There is more mystery involved in our understanding of how the movie was made than there is in the movie itself. Chambers' photos have been dispersed, and it is not certain that a visual record of the disguises survives anywhere but in the finished movie. Many of the scenes of Douglas in disguise are in fact ones in which his stand-in, Jan Merlin, is wearing his faces, and there is little consensus about which scenes are which. Moreover, some of the ostensible appearances of Lancaster and perhaps others in disguise are also said to be of stand-ins. The effectiveness of the disguises in *Adrian Messenger* could have been enhanced had the movie been in color, but Chambers' desires were overruled by Huston, who did not altogether trust the makeup process, and the finished movie is in black and white.

Several other well-received movies of midcentury relied on disguise plots. *Witness for the Prosecution*, Billy Wilder's 1957 adaptation of Agatha Christie's story, gives Marlene Dietrich the opportunity to carry off a crucial disguise convincingly. But as testimony to the wizardry of makeup, the achievement is compromised by the fact that the disguise works through contrivances of shadow and distance. Anthony Schaffer's play, *Sleuth*, adapted as a movie in 1972 with Michael Caine and Laurence Olivier, also features disguise. The story unfolds as a series of practical jokes and games between a mystery novelist and a travel agent (a hairdresser in the play) after the novelist discovers that the younger man is having an affair with his wife. The movie never escapes (or even tries to escape) the confines and structure of the play. Although Caine's character fools us when he appears as a Scotland Yard inspector in baldcap and wig, with false nose and lens, the disguise's persuasiveness owes as much to a fake accent and the diversions of dialogue as it does to makeup.

Hardly any more recent well-known movies have given the same kind of attention to disguise. *Happy New Year* (1973), a typically French meld of crime and romance, makes effective use of disguises, as does its American remake (1987) with Peter Falk. But in the original, the camera suspiciously keeps its distance from the disguised protagonist, and closeups reveal rough sculpting and exaggerated features.

The most dazzling examples of prosthetic disguises in recent movies and television dramas were created for projects that were hardly noticed. For contemporary makeup artists, that tends to be the rule. The quality of their work has little to do with the quality or importance of the surrounding story, and the opportunities for wizardry are few.

We saw that, since it is easy to carry out a rape, homicide, or bank robbery unrecognized, most criminals would hardly need elaborate prosthetic disguises. One would have to be crazy to think otherwise. And an exotic, only-for-television brand of craziness distinguishes two television psychopaths. The dark and moody television series *Profiler* featured, in its first two seasons, as its protagonist Sam(antha) Waters, an FBI psychologist who is stalked by a serial killer known only as "Jack-of-all-trades." Having killed Sam's husband, Jack plays out an obsessive life-and-death game with Samantha, tormenting her by killing persons important in her life, and daring her to uncover his identity and bring him to justice. Jack, more an artifact of television than reality, sustains an aura of menace around Sam. The notion of interminable pursuit echoes such series as *The Fugitive* and *The Prisoner*. The audience is hooked by Sam's predicament only as long as Jack's identity remains a mystery, even as the audience, like Sam, wants to believe that it is getting closer to endgame.

In an essential *Profiler* episode, Jack finally reveals himself—or so we think. He contrives to meet Sam's lover, Coop, in a train station, intending (perhaps) to kill him. Gnarled, balding, the very image of a fifty-something hardcase with the cadence of the rural South, he toys with Coop and the camera, until he excuses himself and, in the seclusion of the men's room, strips off his face. Filmed in extreme closeup, the

Figure 6.1. Dennis Christopher

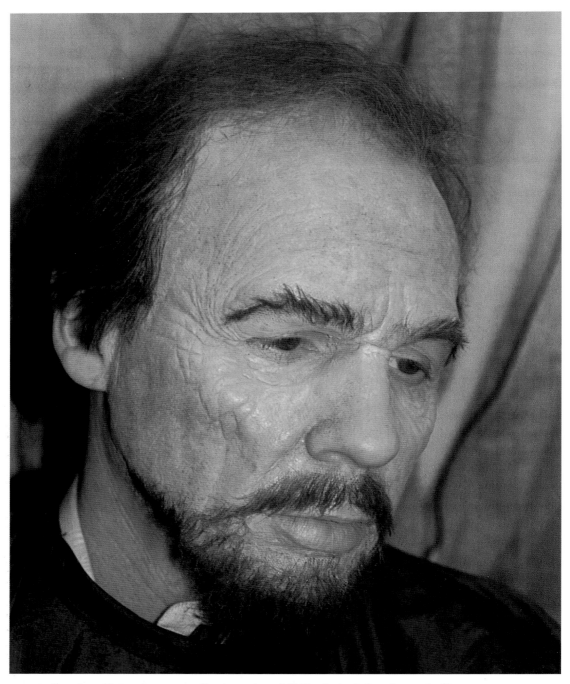

Figure 6.2. Christopher wears a disguise as the serial killer, Jack-of-all-trades, on *Profiler*. Makeup by Todd Masters/MastersFX.

unmasking gives nothing away of Jack's appearance. The disguise itself, executed by Todd Masters on Dennis Christopher, who plays Jack in a continuing role, is masterful.

The notion that psychopaths, rather than other killers, will resort to elaborate disguises because they are wracked by questions of identity is supported by other examples. In the serial *The Guiding Light* a recent plot had Brent Lawrence, a convicted rapist, seeking revenge on his accuser/victim. His complex if improbable scheme was to assume the character of a middle-aged and self-pitying female office worker named Marian Crane, and gain the confidence of his once-and-future victim. It is made clear, to the extent that murky psychological clichés can be made clear, that his disguise has much to do with his psychotic identification with his own absent mother.

Notwithstanding a plot as tenuously connected to reality as Brent himself, the disguise had to be persuasive. The makeup, applied by makeup artist Norman Bryn to Frank Beaty, the actor who is Brent/Marian, works remarkably well on several levels. Beaty is unrecognizable, and his acting is convincing. The new face looks real, and it embodies the demeanor of a profoundly sour and irremediably plain middle-aged woman. If the face looks waxy and artificial, it only shows the vain struggles of an unattractive woman to camouflage her looks with ineptly used cosmetics.

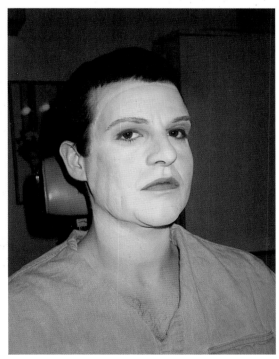

Figure 6.3. Frank Beaty

Figure 6.4. Beaty on the way to becoming "Marian Crane." Makeup by Norman Bryn.

Figure 6.5. "Marian Crane" as portrayed by Frank Beaty on *The Guiding Light*. Makeup by Norman Bryn.

The notion that those using elaborate prosthetic disguises marks a profound disturbance about one's identity is also suggested by a seductive, little-known mystery drama released only on cable and video, *Chameleon*. Anthony LaPaglia is indisputably on the right side of the law as Willie Serling, an undercover drug agent. Having suffered the loss of his young wife and child at the hands of sadistic drug traffickers, he is (the screenwriter insists) in full flight from his life, willing and anxious to assume any identity but his own. The role gives LaPaglia unlimited opportunities to try out accents, costumes, personae, and four impenetrable disguises. The disguises play a small part in advancing the plot, giving Serling opportunities to manipulate circumstances; they matter more as manifestations of his angst than as tools of his trade.

Virtually unknown, *Chameleon* is a disarming success in two ways. Kevin Haney's transformations of LaPaglia are state-of-the-art accomplishments. Each—the homeless black man, the pony-tailed computer technician, the old political demonstrator, and the street-person—retains the basic configuration of LaPaglia's features with enough thickening here, heightening there, roughening elsewhere to make him unrecognizable. In each case, his face is fully concealed by the thinnest of prosthetics. In turn, LaPaglia has a field day running through a lexicon of actors' techniques, slipping in and out of accents, in and out of emotional states.

The makers of *Chameleon* flirted with the idea of having Serling always appear in disguise, never as his own recognizable self, to dramatize his inability to live inside his own skin. This idea was quickly jettisoned, and LaPaglia's undercover identities are for the most part variations of himself; the four thorough disguises appear only in brief sequences. But Serling's superiors express genuine and growing concern that he is losing his sanity, that he is

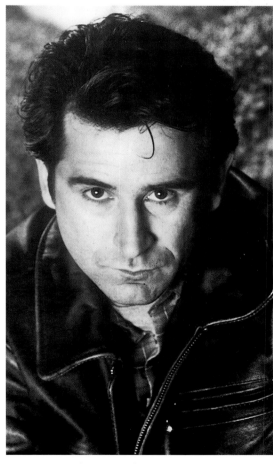

Figure 6.6. Anthony LaPaglia

Figures 6.7, 6.8, 6.9, 6.10 (this page and next). Various disguises used by Willie Serling, LaPaglia's character in *Chameleon*. Makeup by Kevin Haney.

suffering a psychotic implosion of personality. Very little of this is manifested in Serling's actions, which are those of a rational and efficient undercover agent.

Chameleon, like *Profiler* and *The Guiding Light*, is at pains to explain its character's penchant for disguise by appeal to psychological crises of identity. If circumstances do not require so elaborate a transformation, the identity problems of the character do. In all such cases, there must be a coherent account of the pains the character takes to achieve his disguise.

A different route of explaining a character's use of disguise is to fall back on the staple of myths, magical or at least supernatural powers. A supernatural account, in the form of alien technology, gives Todd Masters the occasion to create an utterly convincing disguise for Charlie Sheen in *The Arrival*. It seems that alien beings, long resident in a fortified habitat miles below the earth's surface, have devices that effectively give them the appearance of humans. Transformed, they have infiltrated our government and other institutions. Sheen's character, stumbling upon the aliens' subterranean facilities, is in flight from them when he finds their transformation ma-chines. He adopts the look of a His-panic worker and blends in with a group of other enslaved workers. (We are spared an account of how the technology works, and of why for example Sheen does not end up looking like the aliens.) Fortunately for Sheen's character, the process seems to be reversible.

Sheen's disguise is so thorough that, in a sense, it backfires for the audience. One easily assumes that, in the familiar fraudulent style of the old *Mission: Impossible* show, another actor had been substituted for Sheen. Even sustained scrutiny of photos of Todd Masters' extraor-dinary prosthetic makeup barely dispels our incredulity.

Sometimes, as in myths, the tech-nology of transformation does not have to be explained in the plot. Su-pernatural characters, even in natu-ral settings, may have inherent pow-

Figure 6.11. Charlie Sheen

Figure 6.12. In *The Arrival*, Sheen's character assumes an alien disguise. Makeup by Todd Masters/MastersFX.

Figures 6.14, 6.15, 6.16, 6.17 (this page and next). Feore's character, Andre Linoge, has many faces in Stephen King's *Storm of the Century*. Makeup by Dave Dupuis and Adrien Morot for Steve Johnson/XFX Inc.

Figure 6.13. Colm Feore

ers to wear many faces. Such a demonic chameleon is Andre Linoge in Stephen King's *Storm of the Century*. As played in the miniseries by the gifted Canadian actor Colm Feore, Linoge assumes the innocuous look of a thirty-something wanderer, one whose malign intentions and powers slowly become evident as the village he visits discovers it can save itself from destruction only by selling Linoge a child. Eventually the villagers grow certain that this is the devil's bargain, and Linoge's true face—gnarled but ageless, a face empty of mercy—emerges. Throughout the ordeal and after, Linoge plays tricks with the villagers, assuming the faces of a hellfire preacher, a fat reporter, a distinguished elderly man, and so forth.

The artists at Steve Johnson's XFX Inc., specifically Dave Dupuis and Adrien Morot, had a field day with Feore's disguises. Use of foamed gelatin for the old devil makeup was an innovation. The other disguises used more traditional materials, foam latex and ordinary gelatin prosthetics. Not all ambitions were realized. A plan to turn Feore into a seductive woman produced results that were abandoned.

There is a third way to find a place for disguise in a contemporary plot. We saw that one way is to give the character a psychotic concern with identity, and a second (Sheen, Feore) is to provide magical or supernatural powers of transformation. A third possibility recalls Shakespeare's conventions, dramas and comedies that assume a playful, cartoonish attitude toward events and possibilities. They may be more realistic than cartoons, but they preserve the idea of tweaking reality's rules.

Lily in Love (1985) reworks Molnar's play *The Guardsman* and features Maggie Smith and Christopher Plummer as a "royal couple of the English theater." Smith's career is flourishing at the expense of Plummer's. When she rejects him as the leading man of her next play, he takes revenge by disguising himself as an Italian rake, with the double aim of seducing her and winning the part. When he is successful in both, however, one is left with doubt about whether Smith's character has seen through his deception all along.

Carl Fullerton's makeup for Plummer walks a fine line. The appearance of neither the faded English actor nor the Italian arriviste is Plummer unmodified. The first is aged with eyebags and jowls; the latter has a tightened jaw line, a Romanized nose, and the blondest of wigs. Unlike most other disguise examples, the goal here is not unrecognizability. Rather, the character is supposed to be a plausible variation of himself whose disguise works, if it does, only because of his undervalued acting skills. In part the disguise reminds us of the conventions of Elizabethan theater, whereby critical scrutiny of the character is ruled out and the flimsiest of disguises suffices.

Figure 6.18. Christopher Plummer

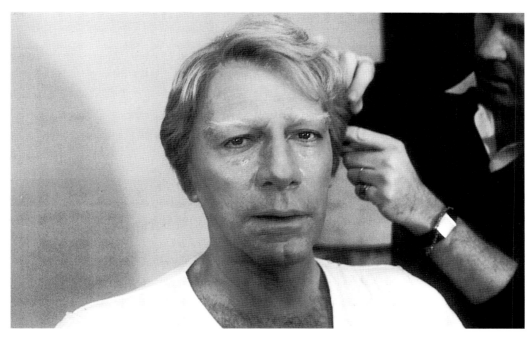

Figures 6.19, 6.20. Carl Fullerton turned Plummer into older and younger variations of himself for *Lily in Love*.

The movie toys with us, playing off different hypotheses about the gullibility of the characters themselves and the conventions by which they live. Are they fooled, as Shakespearean characters might be fooled, or are they playing out a game in which deception by disguise fails to convince a contemporary critical eye? The movie works either way, and Fullerton's clever makeup supports either reading.

Taken together, these various examples of plots involving disguise illustrate a paradox. As the skills of makeup artists have been refined to the point where realistic and convincing disguises are achievable in movies, the need for them has come closer to the vanishing point, for the paradoxical reason that effective disguise, in the common imagination, is dismissed as impossible. Thus, we commonly accept the convention that Bruce Willis can escape a hail of bullets unscathed, or that Jackie Chan can karate-chop an army of villains into submission or incapacity without the kind of damage that slows them down. On the other hand, our eyes and experience tell us that hardly anyone can carry off an effective transformation. The skills and equipment needed are formidable, and the characters in movies are unlikely to have them. And, even if they do, disguises run a high risk of giving themselves away. In this domain, our standards of realism are unforgiving—and at odds with older conventions of theatrical artifice.

Of course, the attitude reflects both good sense and a mystery. The good sense is a correct and realistic assessment of the capacity of even the most skilled makeup artists to carry off disguises outside the controlled context of moviemaking. The mystery is why we happily suspend our insistence on realism in some contexts and not others.

Acting with Multiple Identities

Alec Guinness in *Kind Hearts and Coronets* (1949) was the perfect chameleon. In the story of the homicidal outcast of a titled family, Guinness played all eight members of the family who became the killer's victims, characters of all ages and genders. His feat was unrivaled until Eddie Murphy, drawing on the makeup skills of Rick Baker, perpetrated *Coming to America* and *The Nutty Professor*.

Nothing in the story of *Kind Hearts* requires the victims to be played by one actor. Similarly, nothing about *Coming to America* requires Murphy to play a gossiping barber, an elderly Jewish hanger-on in the barbershop, and a talentless walleyed lounge singer in addition to his main role as an African prince in search of an American bride. The characters have no importance except as vehicles for Murphy's powers as a mimic. Ordinarily, impostures involving disguise exist primarily as plot devices, whereby one character tries to fool other characters (and

Figures 6.21, 6.22, 6.23, 6.24. Eddie Murphy's various characters—an African prince, an elderly Jew, a loquacious barber, and a lounge singer—in *Coming to America.*
Makeup by Rick Baker/Cinovation.

perhaps incidentally fool the audience). Murphy's disguises, on the other hand, exist only to tease the movie's audience—and they work equally well whether one is in on the con or not.

Coming to America has something in common with *The List of Adrian Messenger* insofar as both deconstruct the process of storytelling. Both force us to think about acting and role-playing, about the Protean character of acting in a way that has nothing to do with the unfolding story. Bertolt Brecht's theatrical projects exploit strategies for distancing the audience from plays and making them contemplate the artificiality and malleability of theatrical conventions. Countless performance artists and postmodern theater works have done the same. In its playful way, *Coming to America* taps into the same ideas in celebrating the chameleon nature of the actor.

Crucial to the success of *Coming to America* is the quality of Rick Baker's makeup. The elderly Jewish pedant is the ultimate *gee whiz* creation. One's eyes continue to deny what one knows to be true: "That *can't* be Eddie Murphy." The illusion stuns because of Baker's skill in seeming to reshape the very bone structure of the character; the new face, but not Murphy's, seems narrow, a counterpoint of nose and chin.

For obvious reasons, racial transformation is one of the makeup artist's ultimate tests. Every race has characteristic features nearly impossible to camouflage—Asian eyes, the long Caucasian nose, the fleshy lips of the African. We have already seen the paradox of the makeup artist's illusions, namely that addition must look like subtraction if the invented face is not to look unnatural. With racial transformation, the complications are multiplied.

In *The Nutty Professor* Murphy and Baker reprise their achievement with a "more is better" conviction. Murphy plays more unrecognizable characters (count 'em: six), Baker pulls out all the stops in transforming his star, and the main character himself could hardly be bigger. Murphy plays not only Sherman Klump, the voluminous protagonist, the proverbial gentle giant, but members of the Klump family of various ages and genders. It is hard to fault the acting. The Oscar-winning makeup is equally fine. Baker's work here is a lexicon of techniques, with thin and delicate rubber appliances used for Murphy as mother Klump, a thicker prosthetic mask for Sherman's heavy-featured brother, and pouches of fluid encased in rubber for Sherman's quavery multiple chins.

In two ways, *The Nutty Professor* is less subversive than *Coming to America*. The racial crossover character in *Nutty*, Murphy as a clone of Richard Simmons, the exercise guru for geriatrics, is not really persuasive, with a face that looks something like a racial salad. And *Nutty* doesn't quite trick the audience into deconstructing the art of acting. We are all clued in to the metamorphoses of Eddie Murphy, and we are no more deceived than by any other highwire act.

Actors such as Guinness and Murphy are special, chameleons impatient with the limitations of ordinary roles in mere stories. The trick realized in *Kind Hearts* and *Coming to America* must be rationed. Disguise works only by fooling persons, whether those fooled are other characters in the story or, in these extraordinary circumstances, audiences that expect actors to wear their own

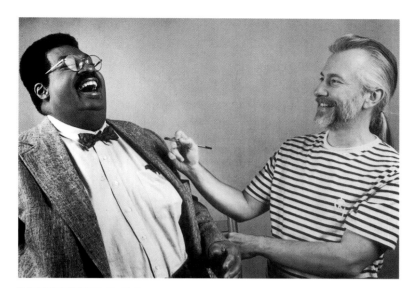

Figures 6.25, 6.26, 6.27, 6.28, 6.29 (this page and p. 144). *The Nutty Professor* gave Murphy the chance to play most members of the Klump family: Sherman, his brother, grandmother, father, and mother. Makeup by Rick Baker/Cinovation.

faces, or at least one consistent face. The trick palls with familiarity, as the audience for *The Nutty Professor* comes to expect metamorphosis as the norm.

Disguise as State of the Art

There is a gap between the makeup artist's skills and ambitions, on the one hand, and his opportunities. Doing *Coming to America* or *The Nutty Professor* is a rare chance, and Rick Baker is lucky to have had it twice, luckier still to be in a position to generate more such projects. Even more modest opportunities are also rare. Few makeup artists get to turn a Frank Beaty into a Marian Crane *(Guiding Light)* or Anthony LaPaglia into a man of many faces *(Chameleon)*.

Eager to exploit their art in its purest form, makeup artists sometimes devise projects "for the portfolio," demonstrations done for their own sake. The goal here is to explore the state of the art, to show how extreme a transformation can be, radical and convincing at the same time. Doing it is its own justification. (Asked why he climbed the mountain, the climber replied, "Because it was there.") And there are other motives. A portfolio exits less for narcissistic con-

Figure 6.31. Kevin Yagher made Alec Gillis into a much-weathered homeless man.

Figure 6.30. Alec Gillis

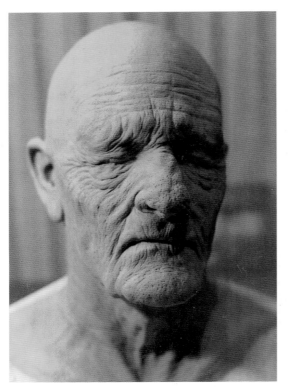

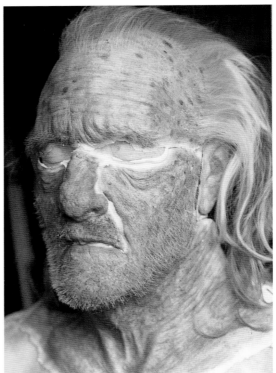

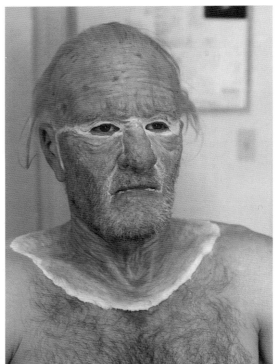

Figures 6.32, 6.33, 6.34. The sculpture, prosthetic appliances, and appliances-as-applied for Yagher's transformation of Gillis.

templation than for showing others one's magic, a tool for building and cementing careers.

Kevin Yagher and Alec Gillis have for some time flourished in their own studios, Kevin Yagher Creations and Gillis' (and Tom Woodruff's) ADI. Prosthetic transformations are but one weapon in their arsenal. At the opposite extreme from face creation, Yagher conceived and created the Gremlins (from the movie of the same name), and ADI produced the effects for *Jumanji* and *Alien Resurrection*. But in the 1980s, Yagher and Gillis both worked at Stan Winston's studio. Early in the 1980s, Yagher executed for his portfolio a state-of-the-art age makeup on Gillis that was widely discussed, widely copied. The aim was not so much to conceive Gillis' appearance as an old man as to improvise a character with features of its own, with a distinctive and troubled history engraved in its

Figure 6.35. Steve Johnson created this elderly black woman as a demonstration makeup.

Figure 6.36. The model for Johnson's elderly black woman.

Figures 6.37, 6.38, 6.39 (this page and opposite). Stages in the evolution of Johnson's demo.

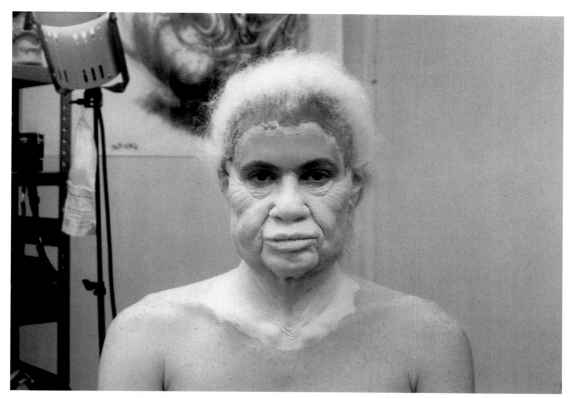

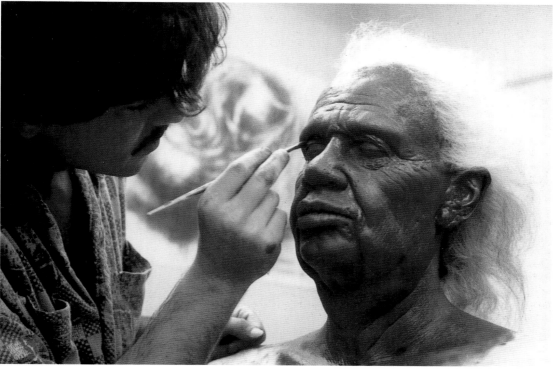

creases and crags. An extraordinary aspect of the makeup was the way in which the gray stubble of the character's beard was secured and anchored, hair by hair, in the prosthetic jowls and chin.

Another makeup demonstration, this one by Steve Johnson, was done for a Japanese book on the art of makeup. Daring himself to invent the most extreme transformation imaginable (given the limited resources of prosthetic appliances), Johnson turned a young white male into an elderly black woman blinded by cataracts. Again, the pictures speak for themselves. Johnson tries to express a personal history, a set of attitudes and experiences within the parameters of a new physiognomy.

Since Johnson was creating his character only for the still camera, he had leeway. The face did not have to move or speak. Johnson could control and limit the lighting of the photographs. One may have misgivings that the thickness of the prosthetic, made necessary by the radicalness of the change, would prevent the face from moving convincingly and being expressive. But makeup artists emphasize that every prosthetic makeup is a compromise with the limitations of the medium, and no project mimics real flesh and real movement in all lights and circumstances. Johnson's project remains exciting as a portrait in rubber.

One of the outstanding foreign craftsmen of makeup is Göran Lundström, whose Effects Studio is in Stockholm. Prominent in Lundström's portfolio is a transformation of Thomas Gylling, who is popular as a Swedish talk show host. For a skit on Swedish television, Lundström used beautifully sculpted foam latex to turn Gylling into an old man with a grandly expressive face.

Espionage

Disguises have a place in movies about criminals, undercover agents, and spies because, as most of us assume, they are used in the actual contexts of crime and espionage. The extent to which this is so can be a closely guarded secret. Both the police and the intelligence service have an understandable interest in keeping their methods to themselves.

What relevance does the work of Hollywood makeup artists have for American intelligence activities? Some, John Chambers for example, consulted with the CIA in the 1970s. It was rumored that the CIA had its own research laboratory, a facility that developed prosthetic masks as disguises more sophisticated than anything Hollywood had to offer.

Antonio Mendez, who ran the CIA's disguise operations for much of the 1980s, is now retired and, with the agency's consent and blessing, has begun giving interviews about his work. Mendez recently published an account of his adventures. Much information is, of course, still classified. It seems clear, however,

Figure 6.40. Thomas Gylling (Swedish talk show host)

Figure 6.41. Gylling in the process of becoming a senior citizen. He is being transformed by makeup assistant Erik Møystad, wigmaker Jenny Martinpelto, and make-up artist Göran Lundström.

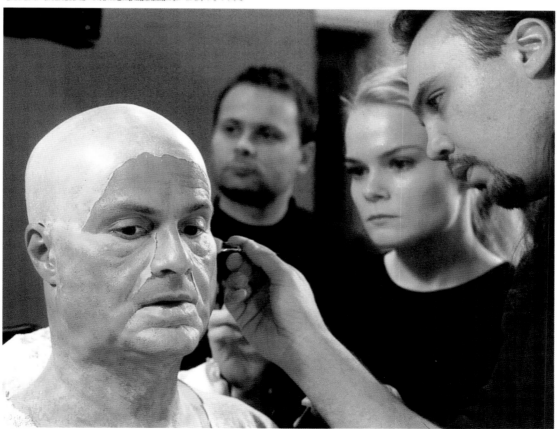

Figure 6.42. Gylling fully transformed. Makeup by Göran Lundström/Effects Studio. Hairwork by Jenny Martinpelto and Katrin Wahlber.

that Mendez and his associates advanced the state of the art of makeup. A variation of the old *Mission: Impossible* ideal was to create and use an entirely convincing false face that could be applied and removed almost instantaneously and would be reusable. Nothing in today's Hollywood arsenal meets that ideal. And yet the CIA's lab seems to have developed and used new materials with the aspiration to achieve such results.

In an interview with Mr. Mendez, I asked why the CIA, building in part on Hollywood's own experience, might have outdistanced the movie industry. The suggestive response was that the movies have never needed to do what may be essential to an intelligence agent's safety and survival. Transformational effects in the movies can be prepared over several hours. Lighting and camera angles can always be controlled. New prosthetic pieces can be prepared for each application. The agent in the field under surveillance has none of these options.

The preparation of realistic false faces was a small part of the CIA's expertise in disguise. Fooling an observer and adopting camouflage requires many skills and is necessary in varying contexts. Sometimes a new way of dressing or walking and gesturing will suffice to throw off scrutiny. Being disguised is as much a matter of psychology, of acting with conviction when one may never have had to act before, as it is a matter of wearing a false face. Mendez and his associates had to cover all these bases.

Interface

Thinking in general about disguise leads to questions about the means and ends of transformational makeup. We are in the habit of thinking of the art of transformation as a means. In myth and philosophical imagination, *actual* transformation—trading one's old body for a new one—is a means to immortality. In practical imagination, it is a means to fool others, to eavesdrop or play dirty tricks undetected. In the actual practice of transformational makeup artists, it is a means for producing demons and aliens on demand, for resurrecting Genghis Khan or Mark Twain, for portraying a single life from youth to extreme age.

But when we focus on disguise, it matters less what one becomes and more that one is no longer oneself. Transformation becomes largely an end in itself, a way of escaping from, toying with, and manipulating identity. Characters in movies need or want to put their own identity at arm's length. Actors such as Eddie Murphy seize opportunities to show their versatility, to be chameleons. And makeup artists themselves, like Kevin Yagher, Steve Johnson, and Göran Lundström, strain to show us not so much what their magical processes can yield but rather that the processes themselves have no limits, that makeup artists can in fact play God.

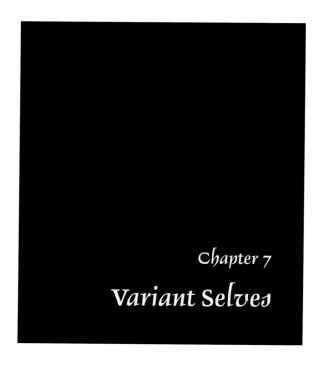

O wad some Pow'r the giftie gie us
To see oursels as others see us!
It wad frae mony a blunder free us,
and foolish notion.

ROBERT BURNS, "To a Louse"

Learning from Mirrors

Psychologists note that most of us cannot recognize our own voice. The same is not true for faces. Most of us have no trouble picking ourselves out in a photograph. The reason is clear. We have almost no occasions to hear our voices the way others do, from outside ourselves. But we do see our faces as part of the world of objects, in mirrors for example.

But do we, as Burns asks, "see ourselves as others see us"? The psychological evidence suggests that self-perception is likely to be distorted. We all know about the extreme pathologies. Anorexics cannot help but see themselves as fat. Others—pleasant looking, even handsome—may avoid social contact in the belief that they are revoltingly ugly.

Are these the rare emotionally disturbed unfortunates in a society of healthy persons who see themselves veridically? Or are they the extremes of a spectrum along which all the rest of us lie? We are unlikely to answer such questions easily. It is clear, however, that most of us have a greater stake in coming to terms with our *own* appearance than we do with that of others.

Objectifying ourselves is a peculiar process. It remains mysterious, however much it is studied by psychologists and philosophers. Much of Western philosophy takes its marching orders from Descartes and takes for granted that persons are conjunctions of mind and body, minds housed in bodies. Recent philosophers have had doubts about this way of stating matters, suggesting that the relationship is not simply between two entities that happen to be joined, not comparable *either* to the way in which a table and a chair both occupy the same room, *or* to the way a person lives within a house. The metaphors (for mind and body) of coexistence and habitation may both be misleading.

However one poses the issue, our bodies, which *are* physical objects in the world, are very special objects to us. Our consciousness seems to depend on our bodies existing and flourishing. Our ways of being treated depend on how our bodies are seen and judged by others. Thus, it seems natural to have a significant preoccupation with the body's well-being and appearance. Only persons with uncommon spiritual beliefs are likely to abstract themselves from such concerns.

How well do we know our appearance? Most of us have no trouble keeping in mind objective facts: our height, weight, hair color and distribution, skin color, distinguishing marks such as scars and moles. But can we summon up a mental image of ourselves in the way that we can picture our friends? Can we judge whether we "look our age" from the evidence in the mirror, as we can (for the most part) in judging others? Can we arrive at a stable esthetic opinion about ourselves, regardless of how comfortable we are with that opinion?

It is plausible that the special role of our bodies invests these judgments with emotional importance and, perhaps, volatility. We may exaggerate variations in our looks ("I've aged ten years in the last month." "This pimple, this scar ruins my looks." "Today I don't look like myself at all.") in ways we hardly ever do with others.

It is also true that we live with our bodies all our lives and experience the body's variations over time. With a little imagination and a lot of nostalgia, we contrast our middle-aged looks with our selves when young. Those who have gained or lost weight, or suffered change through a disfiguring injury or plastic surgery, or simply aged, may constantly have in mind both present and past selves. We can hardly estimate, or *over*estimate, the persistence of memory, the way our current self-perception is colored by memories of what we were.

Do we ever fail to recognize ourselves? Again, it's hard to know. Looking in a mirror is purposeful, and the immediacy of eye contact is sufficient to forestall confusion. But perhaps we have all had the experience of looking at unusually angled mirrors, perhaps a mirror reflecting us in a group in unexpected ways, to be caught unaware in a delayed reaction of "Oh my God, that's me." The same may happen if one stumbles on an old photo. Both settings elicit the fleeting and evanescent experience of self-objectification.

An actor radically transformed into an alien, demon, or historical figure will have a unique interest in mirrors. It will be normal for him to fail to recognize himself, just as he will anticipate that others will not recognize him. Responses that might warn of psychosis or supernatural intervention in another setting are the norm in this particular context. Moreover, there are continuities within discontinuities. Actors sometimes claim that they get used to their new faces. Makeup technicians, costume persons, directors, and other actors persist in speaking to them as their familiar selves, ignoring the transformation. In this sense looking altogether different is just an ordinary part of the workday of otherwise normal continuities and expectations.

And yet actors may also find the experience unsettling. If they are in makeup all day every day for the duration of their role, they may never meet their fellow actors wearing their real faces. In such cases, others may by default treat them as having the characteristics (age, attractiveness, disabilities) of their characters. And many never get accustomed to the uncanny message that the mirror seems to send.

Oneself, but Different

Some roles require a partial transformation that may be much more unsettling than a total makeover. The *real* physical transformations that all of us undergo are typically gradual, from youth to old age, from one size and shape to another. Sudden changes are usually catastrophic, a change in weight and appearance brought on by severe illness or disfigurement through accident and injury.

Actors may take their character through such common transformations. A familiar ploy for storytellers is to have a character reflect on his or her life from old age. Another is to glimpse the character at different times over a long and tangled life. More exotic and specialized plots may involve natural or supernatural transformations in shape; one may diet or gorge oneself, or one may be the victim of a mysterious spell that precipitates drastic weight gain or loss. War stories often involve radical injuries that leave permanent marks.

Makeup artists see movies and television dramas that involve such transformations as their personal Everest. Here the art must really be covert, an artless achievement that covers its own tracks. Unlike demons and aliens, the character cannot look made up. Few of us over the age of five take aliens and demons at (literally) face value. Their looks may have a convincing integrity, but we cannot in principle suspend disbelief completely.

Age makeups, by contrast, should be utterly persuasive. Ideally the intervention of makeup should not even be suggested. Disguise makeups should also be convincing and fully deceptive, but here the makeup artist has the freedom to create *any* look as long as it distracts us from the actor's real appearance. Age makeups, by contrast, cannot disguise the character into unrecognizability. We must see the resemblance along with the change.

If age makeups are subtler than other projects, they also impose other specialized demands on makeup artists. They require knowledge of the physiology of aging: of how and why cells deteriorate, wrinkles appear, cheeks become hollow, hair recedes and coarsens, jowls collapse, and skinfolds form. They require an understanding of the trajectory of the character's life, of how the adventures, cares and adversities, joys and indulgences of the character's unique history are likely to etch themselves in his or her appearance. Ideally we should be able to read a history in a face, perhaps even more effectively and certainly than we can in real life. Finally, such makeups require technical skill. The prosthetic pieces must be thin and delicate. In many cases, they must create the illusion of *subtraction*, of a face that has begun to collapse in on itself, has lost its firmness and developed hollows and folds.

The difficulties of age makeup make it a field for experimentation. In the last few years, several artists, frustrated with the limitations of foam latex appliances, have tried new or once-rejected materials. Gordon Smith, at FXSmith in Toronto, has become known for his work with appliances made from silicone rubber materials. Others, such as Matthew Mungle and Steve Johnson's team at XFX Inc., have had significant success with gelatin processed in sophisticated ways. In both cases, the advantage is translucency. Silicone and gelatin, being semitransparent, allow the actor's skin to show through the appliance. The result has the appearance of depth, the natural appearance of skin. It reflects light in a way that mimics the properties of skin, and it tends to move, wrinkle, and fold convincingly.

Achieving these effects with foam latex is an uphill battle. Because latex appliances are opaque and cover the skin completely, the illusion of translucency and the naturalness of flesh must be created with layers of color applied to the surface of the rubber and the uncovered parts of the actor's face (if any). The illusion is fragile, readily undermined when the surface reflects light too uniformly or is too shiny or not shiny enough, equally undermined by stretches of "skin" that move in way that human muscles and flesh never can.

The new materials have their own perils. Silicone rubber prosthetics are hard to attach and may need new kinds of adhesives. It is hard as well to blend the edges of such prosthetics invisibly into the actor's skin. While the most convincing foam latex transformations involve multiple thin pieces with edges erased through liberal use of liquid latex, silicone rubber makeups have tended to be large pieces that cover the actor's face entirely. It is much easier to control the process of making several small pieces than one large piece. Moreover, makeup artists are still experimenting with coloring silicone appliances. For the most part, coloring agents are not applied to the surface but rather permeate the piece. Additional colors applied to the surface can look artificial.

Gelatin prosthetics have a longer history. In past decades, gelatin materials were rejected as unstable—disintegrating in heat, vulnerable to chemical deterioration because of sweat, and subject to tearing through friction and abrasion. Recent techniques have ameliorated many of these problems, and gelatin appliances are more and more widely used.

Foam latex remains the medium of choice. But whatever the favored medium, certain elements are constant for the makeup artist and the actor. The makeup artist may be tempted to do too much and too little. "Too much" in this case is a failure of design, violation of the constraint that the actor must remain recognizable, that it must be credible that this is the same character. We all have subliminal notions of how real persons age. As we ourselves age and experience our families and friends over the decades, we become adept at looking at a twenty year old and imagining how he would look at fifty, or looking at a sexagenarian and picturing her as a teenager. We learn how hair recedes, how different kinds of bone structures make themselves evident, how different types of skin coarsen or thin. The makeup artist must guess convincingly that *this* is the way the character would age.

Doing too little is also a trap. The job is often not simply an extreme age makeup, taking the actor abruptly from youth to senescence. It may involve taking the character through stages on life's way or simply from youth to middle age. One may think that these less extreme changes can be achieved by modifying one feature—a hairline, a jowl, an eyebag—and leaving others alone. In fact, all of our features age gradually at the same rate; a two-decade change may require as many alterations, slight ones, as a five-decade change. A new eyebag or a receding hairline on an otherwise unchanged twenty-five-year-old actor looks silly.

It is harder to see what special demands these transformations make on the actor. Finding new gestures, a new voice, an appropriate demeanor are the everyday stuff of acting. But with most parts, those that require no radical physical transformation as well as those that do, the actor can often define limits: "This is where I end and the character begins." Faced with the subtlest of age makeups, the actor is likely to find the job of separation hard. The mirror confronts the actor not merely with a new character but with his or her actual self decades down the road. "If I live long enough, this is who I may be" is a realization hardly conducive to keeping oneself and one's roles comfortably distinct.

Making Up for Lost Time

The techniques used for old-age makeup are, for the most part, widely shared. About thirty years ago, Dick Smith revolutionized age makeup. The 1970 movie *Little Big Man* used a framing device whereby 121-year-old Jack Crabb recalls his life in the old west through flashbacks. Dustin Hoffman plays Crabb in old age and youth. Dick Smith's old-age makeup consisted of multiple thin overlapping foam latex appliances that fitted together to cover most, if not all, of the actor's face. This method, refined in such movies as *Amadeus*, was then revolutionary. It has been widely imitated and remains the standard. Smith is revered for sharing his research and techniques.

A persuasive example of an extreme age makeup was created by Michael Westmore and his associates on *Star Trek: Deep Space Nine* for the episode "Distant Voices." Dr. Julian Bashir, played by Siddig El-Fadil (now Alexander Siddig), falls under the spell of alien intelligence. To his colleagues on DS9, he appears in a coma and in imminent danger of losing his life energy. In his mind, he is living his life in fast-forward. His dream/hallucination culminates in a macabre party celebrating his hundredth birthday and impending death. He is required to assess his life as success or failure. Reclaiming his decisions as successes provides the key to emerging from his coma and throwing off the alien influence.

The makeup, following closely on Smith's example, is magically effective in conveying great age. Folds of skin seem collapsed on the underlying skull. The eyes, enhanced with contact lenses, seem sunken in their sockets. The narrowness of Siddig's own face helps Westmore with the illusion of subtraction, that the aged face is withered and thinner than the face of youth.

Not all effective age appliances are sculpted over the actor's own features. Generic pieces can be convincing and often used on low-budget, low-visibility projects. Age makeups, as well as monster and alien creations, occur in TV and print advertisements—and they sometimes use available resources.

Norman Bryn in Norwalk, Connecticut, has built his career as a makeup consultant for soap operas and theater in Manhattan. His age makeup for a pharmaceuticals ad campaign uses generic pieces to take his model from about thirty years to about seventy. The photos show how effectively pieces created for other

Figure 7.1. Alexander Siddig

Figure 7.2. Siddig aged to 100 in the episode "Distant Voices," for *Star Trek: Deep Space Nine*. Makeup by Michael Westmore's team at Paramount.

Figure 7.3. Norman Bryn's age makeup for a pharmaceutical ad.

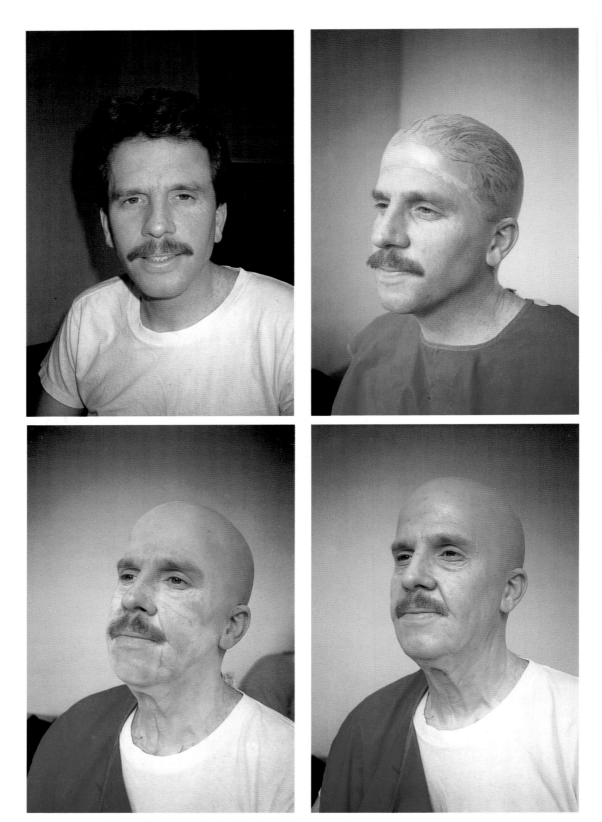

Figures 7.4, 7.5, 7.6, 7.7. The stages of aging Bryn's model.

Figure 7.8. The model for an age transformation by Todd McIntosh for a Japanese beer ad.

Figure 7.9. McIntosh's model well-aged.

Figure 7.10. Fionagh Cush (accompanied by a *Babylon 5* Brakiri—actually actor Rick Ryan).

Figure 7.11. Greg Funk transformed Fionagh Cush using photos of her grandmother.

purposes can be appropriated, and how the model's own features can be blended into the prosthetic appliances. At each stage the model's own appearance slips farther away and his aged self comes into focus.

Bryn's project also shows how an age transformation recapitulates a personal history. The face here is somber, thoughtful, and cultured, bearing an old world dignity and sobriety. In a project for a Japanese beer commercial, Todd McIntosh achieved a similarly compelling effect, taking a Caucasian actor from his thirties to his eighties. (One is supposed to be moved by the fact that over fifty years he remained faithful to Black Star beer.) And, for his portfolio, Greg Funk took Fionagh Cush a half century into her future, using photos of her grandmother as a template.

By contrast, Todd Masters' old-age makeups often suggest characters with troubled pasts and limited futures. Masters worked for several seasons on the series *Tales from the Crypt*, a series in which the few characters who survived to old age could rarely be said to have lived without regrets. In "Staired in Horror," D. B. Sweeney plays a criminal who gets his just desserts in a predictably ironic way when he hides in a decrepit mansion inhabited by a crone. The old woman is in fact young and glamorous but has been placed under a spell by the husband she betrayed. And residents of the house are vulnerable to the same spell. Sweeney's face in old age shows the ravages of time and circumstance. Abraham Lincoln (or perhaps Edwin Stanton, the authorities are unsure) said that "by the age of fifty, we are all responsible for our faces."

A more benign fate is in the cards for an aged version of country singer Travis Tritt, created by Todd Masters for a music video. The twenty-something Tritt is propelled forward into a plausible version of himself—or perhaps his grandfather—five decades in the future. His look belongs to a timeless rural American, just shy of Norman Rockwell.

Equally radical, if more generic, age makeups were designed by Masters for Eric Close as John Loengard, hero of the short-lived science fiction series *Dark Skies*, and Joanna Kerns for the television movie *Emma's Wish*. *Dark Skies* took place at the start of the Cold War when fears of nuclear annihilation were fresh and raw. Loengard, living through the 1950s and 1960s as a sometime-renegade government agent, finds evidence that government agencies, in cooperation with the military, are covering up and exploiting secret contacts with extraterrestrials. He risks being silenced as he tries to discover the truth and expose the cover up. *E. T.* meets *The X-Files* with more than a pinch of *JFK* paranoia. In any case, one episode presumes that the protagonist has survived into old age to look back on his life from well into the new millennium.

Masters, who has experimented successfully with computer techniques, developed his age makeup for Close initially using a computer model rather than clay

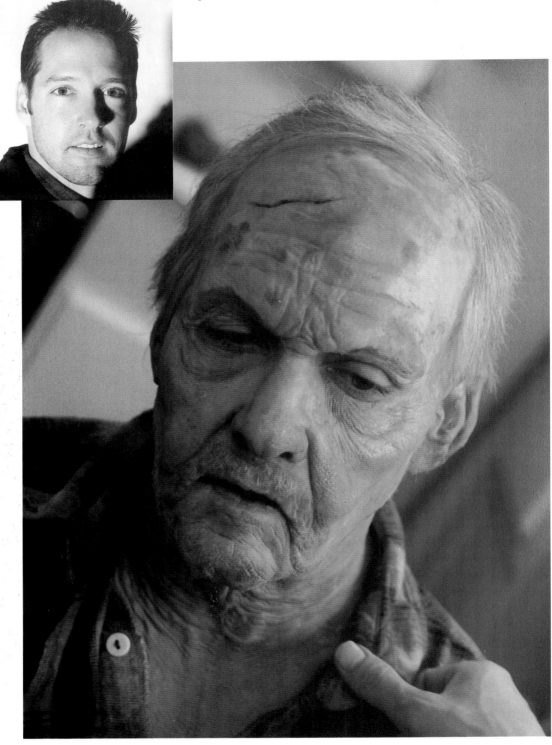

Figure 7.12. D. B. Sweeney

Figure 7.13. D. B. Sweeney ages badly in an episode of *Tales from the Crypt*. Makeup by Todd Masters/MastersFX.

Figure 7.14. Travis Tritt

Figure 7.15. For a music video, Todd Masters turned Travis Tritt into his own grandfather.

Figure 7.16. Eric Close

Figure 7.17. An episode of *Dark Skies* required Eric Close to flash forward more than three decades. Makeup by Todd Masters/MastersFX.

to sculpt a new look. The process has its limits when, as in this case, it produces an aged character with hollowed cheeks and brow. Prosthetics cannot achieve this, of course, unless the actor loses much weight. In this case the final makeup, convincing as it is, retains the contours of Close's own face.

Emma's Wish offers a convincingly subtle transformation. The story gives an elderly resident of a nursing home the chance to re-enter and change her world with youth restored. The makeup allows Joanna Kerns to inhabit both stages of the character with uncommon grace and conviction.

For *The Golden Years*, a miniseries based on a Stephen King novel, Carl Fullerton had the disconcerting job of making his main actor younger, much younger. The character, a janitor in a nuclear facility, is affected by toxins in a way that reverses the aging process. As the story proceeds, he moves from comfortable old age to restless youth. For Fullerton, the foam latex makeup on Keith Szarabajka had to be as convincing as possible since nothing in the early part of the story, largely about the settled life of an elderly couple, could give away the actual mismatch in age of the actors.

Old Faces, New Materials

Because age makeups are the subtlest and most unforgiving of makeup tasks, they are the experimental frontier for new materials and techniques. Although nothing threatens to displace foam latex appliances as the material of choice, makeup artists in the last decade have had successes on three fronts: adapting silicone gels to create convincing prosthetic appliances, reconstituting gelatin to give it the durability needed for prosthetics, and reformulating latex recipes to mimic skin more effectively than ever.

Gordon Smith, at FXSmith in Toronto, moved to makeup after working as an actor and director. Lacking the traditional apprenticeship of other makeup artists, he never developed proficiency with foam latex and thus never took it for granted

Figure 7.18. Joanna Kerns

Figure 7.19. In *Emma's Wish*, Kerns' elderly character is magically allowed to re-enter her youth. Makeup by Todd Masters/ MastersFX.

Figure 7.20. Keith Szarabajka

Figure 7.21. Carl Fullerton turned Szarabajka into a credibly aged janitor who gets progressively younger in Stephen King's *Golden Years*. Makeup applied by Neal Martz.

as the preferred medium. All of his work to date has been with silicone rubber gels. Given the material's skinlike translucency and texture, Smith's notable successes have been with makeups that most need to efface themselves, age makeups and historical figures. (See Chapter 8 for a discussion of historical figures.)

The movie *Legends of the Fall*, adapted from Jim Harrison's novel, is a melodramatic family saga set on the western frontier in the early twentieth century. It pits Brad Pitt as the younger, restless, iconoclastic brother (Tristan Ludlow) against Aidan Quinn as his older, more conventional sibling (Alfred). Alfred marries a young enchantress who loves, once and forever, the romantic Tristan. The film flashes forward about sixty years through the eyes of Tristan's friend and companion, a Native American called One Stab. Gordon Tootoosis plays One Stab both at the age of forty and after he becomes a carnival attraction at the age of one hundred. Gordon Smith's age makeup for Tootoosis is extravagantly successful in realizing the contours and textures of extreme old age.

Equally convincing is a private portfolio project by the makeup artists at Almost Human, a small studio in Culver City. Pierre Thévènin, one of the artists, used silicone prosthetics to transform himself into an aged, worn, and intimidating version of himself. Thévènin (who has since left Almost Human) works almost exclusively with silicone.

Like Gordon Smith, Matthew Mungle specializes in the subtlest transformations, age and historical characters. But unlike Smith, he has worked in Hollywood for most of the 1980s and 1990s on all kinds of projects: television series, major and minor films, and commercials. Several of his most compelling age transformations, using both refined versions of foam latex and gelatin appliances, have been for low-visibility projects that disappeared without a trace.

For a television production in Hong Kong, Mungle aged the actor Tony Leung. Here he is responsive to racial differences in aging. Just as Asian features

Figure 7.22. Gordon Tootoosis

Figure 7.23. *Legends of the Fall* gave Gordon Smith the chance to use silicone makeup appliances to turn Gordon Tootoosis into a century-old Native American.

Figure 7.24. Pierre-Olivier Thévènin

Figure 7.25. Thévènin and his associates at Almost Human used silicone appliances to give him the marks of a long, hard life.

Figure 7.26. Tony Leung

Figure 7.27. Matthew Mungle aged Tony Leung for a movie in Hong Kong.

Figures 7.28, 7.29. This model, David Muxlow, portrayed more than one member of a family—all attending a reunion in Mitsubishi cars. Makeup by Matthew Mungle.

are characteristically different from Caucasian ones, the ways in which Asian faces age are distinctive. The features tend to tighten, with delicate lines and soft hollows.

Part of Mungle's expertise is in knowing that all features age gradually, that it is at least as challenging to age a person ten years as fifty. The Leung makeup does not involve extreme old age. And another study by Mungle, this one for a Mitsubishi car commercial, takes the model merely from his teens to his forties. The premise of the ad is a family reunion. The family members, all of whom arrive in members of the "family" of Mitsubishi cars, bear an uncanny resemblance to each other. Most, of course, are played by the

Figure 7.30. Richard Dean Anderson

same actor. His last incarnation is in early middle age. What Mungle captures with uncanny skill is both how much is changed in the actor's appearance and how little is changed. In fact, only the tip of the nose and the upper lip survive unmodified.

More than most makeup artists, Mungle has been successful with gelatin-based prosthetics, using them most effectively in his *Ghosts of Mississippi* make-up for James Woods (see Chapter 8). But others have become reluctant converts. Michael Pearce has devised new formulas for foamed gelatin, and Dave Dupuis at Steve Johnson's XFX Inc. has used it with remarkable success to age Richard Dean Anderson. Anderson's cable series, *Stargate SG-1*, sipping from the same pool of generic plots as *Deep Space Nine*, staged an episode in which the space explorers are vulnerable to rapid, uncontrollable aging. Anderson's character makes it to extreme old age and is near death before the process can be arrested.

Whatever the technique and medium, age makeups, even more than other makeup projects, defy easy description. In the hands of Bryn, Mungle, Masters, and other masters, they are the equivalent of classical portraits, inviting us to read personal character and history in a face. What works cannot, or cannot easily, be reduced to words.

Figures 7.31, 7.32. Rapid aging afflicted Anderson's character on *Stargate SG-1*. Here are two stages in his decline. Makeup by Dave Dupuis and others for Steve Johnson/XFX Inc.

Refiguring and Disfiguring

Cyril Connolly said that "imprisoned in every fat man a thin one is wildly signaling to be let out." In certain cases, that is literally true. Makeup artists must occasionally turn a thin actor fat and must do so without a regimen of whipped cream and cheesecake.

The challenge is hardest when the actor must be altogether recognizable in both incarnations. Impressive as it is, Eddie Murphy's transformation into Sherman Klump (see Chapter 6) does not, and is not intended to, meet that test. No one would assume that Eddie Murphy, or rather Murphy's Buddy Love, is what Klump would become after an all-too-rigorous diet. The transformational potion is more powerful than that; it turns Klump into an altogether different person.

But in *The Santa Clause*, Tim Allen's metamorphosis into the North Pole's best known resident is a plausible version of Allen all the way through. As designed by the artists at ADI (Amalgamated Dynamics Incorporated) and applied by Barry Koper, Allen's foam latex prosthetics take him through stages of the process of bulking and aging. As in Mungle's Mitsubishi commercial, the makeup work takes account of the fact that even an intermediate change requires slight modification of every feature. The early stages of his transformation get as much attention and are as complex as the later ones.

Figure 7.33. Tim Allen with Barry Koper

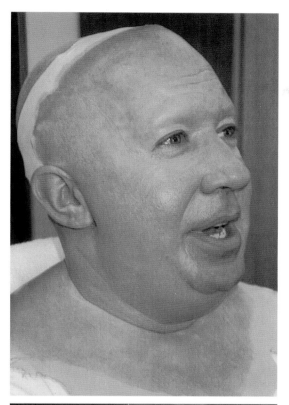

Figures 7.34, 7.35, 7.36. Three stages in Allen's makeup for *The Santa Clause*. Makeup by ADI; applied by Barry Koper.

Koper took special care to blend the colors of the appliances to the tones of Allen's own skin. He avoided, in other words, the common technique of covering everything—both areas of rubber and flesh—with a uniform opaque base color and then seeking the illusion of translucency by adding variations of color and texture on top of the base. Thus, even using foam latex, he achieves a convincing natural look.

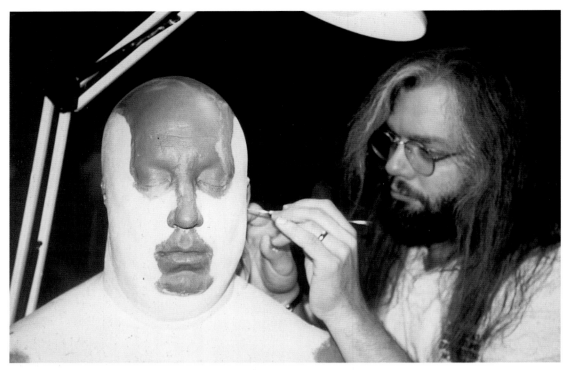

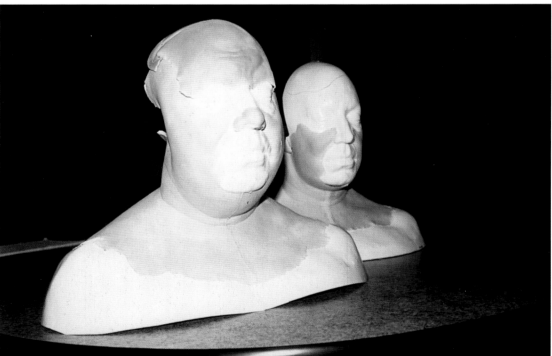

Figures 7.37, 7.38. The delicate prosthetic appliances for *The Santa Clause* were produced by ADI (Amalgamated Dynamics Incorporated).

Figures 7.39, 7.40. An early stage of Allen's aging and bulking-up required extensive makeup. Makeup by ADI; applied by Barry Koper.

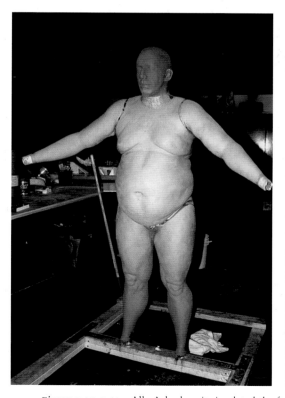
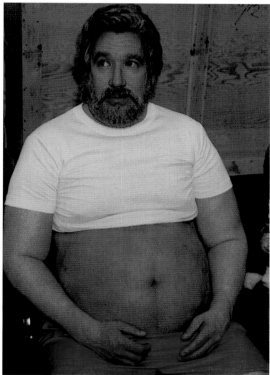

Figures 7.41, 7.42. Allen's body suit simulated the feel and heft of Santa's own girth. Makeup by ADI.

We take the result to be both Tim Allen and Santa Claus without hesitation. The bodily metamorphosis is as innovative as the application of facial prosthetics. Allen's artificial belly has the surface texture, thickness, resiliency, and heft of the belly that the real Santa Claus would come by naturally.

Just as Allen undergoes a radical but highly satisfactory metamorphosis, Alan Cumming in *Romy and Michele's High School Reunion* becomes a physically improved version of himself. The screenplay comments on the fashion of turning so-called computer nerds into the robber barons of the 1990s. Cumming's homely computer genius becomes a handsome man of grace and polish, just barely recognizable thanks to the enhancements of plastic surgery. Kevin Haney's ingenious prosthetic makeup gives him, in Haney's words, "the GQ look."

Not all transformations are as benign as Allen's and Cumming's. In the era before plastic surgery, the wounds of war could be cataclysmically, permanently disfiguring. James Purdy's novel, *In a Shallow Grave*, concerns Garnet Montrose, a young Southerner who returns to his decaying family estate from World War I badly scarred by explosives. His face and much of his body a mass of scar tissue, he retires from society, living a moody existence as a semi-recluse. He hires a rootless young man as his helper, and in particular as go-between with his sometime fiancée.

Michael Biehn plays Montrose in the American Playhouse adaptation of *Shallow Grave*. Michèle Burke's design for Biehn's makeup is stark. It raises immediate questions of identity. We distinguish natural processes

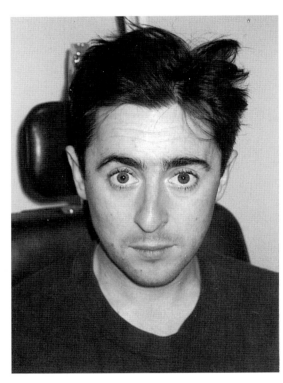

Figure 7.43. Alan Cumming

of transformation—aging, gaining/losing weight—from catastrophic sudden change through violence. The latter sort of change raises a special question: in what sense is someone whose orientation to the world is so thoroughly uprooted still the same person? As Montrose wrestles with this question, the makeup process, both for the actor and the audience, is the physical expression of this dilemma of self-alienation.

Figures 7.44, 7.45. In *Romy and Michele's High School Reunion*, Alan Cumming's character returns to high school glamorized by plastic surgery. Makeup by Kevin Haney.

Figure 7.46. Michael Biehn

Figures 7.47, 7.48. Michèle Burke designed
Biehn's makeup as a veteran disfigured in
World War I for *In a Shallow Grave*.

On Reality and Imagination

The makeup projects in Chapters 4 through 6 untie the imagination. Aliens, demons, disguises all license the makeup artist to remake the actor into a fresh, unrecognizable creation. The actor is reborn with little or no tie to a former self.

The challenge in age and disfigurement makeup, or in transformations for *The Santa Clause*, is take the actor to a variant self. Here the makeup artist must negotiate the constraints of reality, and the actor's natural appearance defines its terms. In recreating characters in history—turning an actor into Mark Twain or Harry Truman—the makeup artist faces a different bargain with reality. He can, in a sense, "lose" the actor, but he must be faithful to the look of the person he is bringing back from the dead, as we will see in Chapter 8.

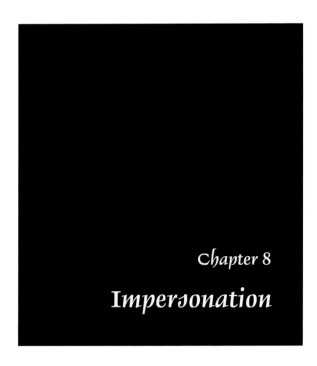

Chapter 8

Impersonation

The actor is not quite a human being—but, then, who is?

GEORGE SANDERS

Impersonation and Crime

Several well-known makeup artists have had meetings with hints of criminal complicity. Strangers approached them, showed pictures of other men, and asked to be disguised as the men in the photos. In each case, the nature of the enterprise was left suspiciously vague. And in each case, the makeup artist, circumspectly and apprehensively, declined.

It is easy to suspect criminal intent. If it is desirable to avoid recognition while committing a crime, it is even better to have someone else positively identified as the criminal. And even apart from criminal conduct, impersonation is the risky business. The dirty tricks of *Mission: Impossible* were carried out in the interest of preventing harm, but they were the kind of morally dubious conduct that government agents had to deny and disclaim.

The movie *Face/Off* is only the latest example of the fantasy of perfect impersonation. The cop and the villain change places, perfectly incarnating each other. As in the television episodes of *Mission: Impossible*, the trick is primarily on the audience as the actors themselves change places; the actor who initially plays the person impersonated also plays the impersonator in disguise. In fact, there is no other way to pull off so exact an impersonation. Makeup alone will not do it.

The makeup artists who declined suspicious offers had more than one reason to refuse. Beyond suspecting that their help might be used for illegal ends, they also knew that their best efforts would fail, that they were being asked to do the impossible. Of course, one *can* impersonate someone else if one can avoid close scrutiny, avoid being asked to speak, and so on. But an impersonation cannot be sustained through a close interaction, especially with someone who knows the person impersonated and is paying attention.

Acting as Biography

Actors are required to become known persons whenever they have to play a biographical role. Some historical figures—Abe Lincoln, Mark Twain, Queen Elizabeth I, Shakespeare, Napoleon, Nixon, and even Elvis Presley—appear over and over again in plays and movies. Generations of actors in the Soviet Union devoted their lives to playing Lenin, living like Tibetan monks (or contemporary skinheads) with their heads shaved. When we think of certain historical figures (Julius Caesar, Cleopatra), our visual referent is of actors most closely associated with the role.

Biographical movies have fallen from popularity. From the 1930s through the 1950s, movie fans were familiar with George Arliss' Disraeli, Henry Fonda's Lincoln, and Marlon Brando's Napoleon. They saw Elizabeth I as Bette Davis' virgin queen and Richard III as a painfully contorted, raven-wigged Laurence Olivier. Biographical films, like other narrative films in the early years of movies, tended to be realistic and naturalistic. Nothing precludes a biographical story from being presented creatively, but it takes a rare imagination to reassemble an actual life into something other than a straightforward chronology. The achievement of *Citizen Kane* is that it subverts and deconstructs this form.

The revolution in film that started in the late 1960s was not congenial to biography. The era of *2001*, *Star Wars*, and *The Godfather* trilogy was inventive and indulgent in its use of extranatural, if not supernatural, effects. Fantasy rather than real life inspired the liberal use of archetypes, irony, and deconstructions of time, space, and human nature. For biography to survive in this climate, it had to be a vehicle for daring special effects, both technical and emotional. It took a *Bonnie and Clyde* to recreate biography in a new key.

A rebirth of conventional storytelling in the 1980s, along with a ruminative kind of muckraking cynicism, was fertile ground for biographical reworkings of recent history. Oliver Stone opted for revisionist history in *JFK* and was more circumspect in *Nixon* and *Born on the Fourth of July*. Films feature cultural icons *(Coal Miner's Daughter, What's Love Got to Do with It?)* and sports figures, especially those who died young and tragically. But biography is hardly a robust genre of contemporary film; the once-common retellings of the lives of Abe Lincoln, Queen Elizabeth I, and Cleopatra are themselves history.

Actors are more often asked to become historical figures—Lincoln, Twain, Hitler, Truman—for television. While no segment of the film market, neither the domain of studio films and would-be blockbusters nor the world of so-called independent film, is particularly hospitable to biographical projects, television is both more conservative and more eclectic. There, biographical movies attract an audience that knows and demands familiarity in content and form. And biographies rarely break budgets or disappoint advertisers.

Biographical acting is a special challenge, and achieving the look of a historical personage is just one demand. Playing fictional characters, actors must follow the words of a writer and the choices of the director, but they need not re-imagine the contours of a lived life. The words and meanings of a playwright or screenwriter are endlessly interpretable, and the demands of directors can be accommodated in different ways. On the other hand, playing an actual person is a different kind of interpretive task, that of inhabiting the thoughts, feelings, actions, and appearance of someone who had a real existence.

The actor thus becomes biographer. The job becomes easy in some ways, hard in others. A well-documented life provides grist for research and thought. The actor does not have to invent a backstory to flesh out the character; a history (or possibly various conflicting histories) is there for the seeking. Distant historical characters are known indirectly; for Caesar or Christ the events of the outer life give clues to the inner life of thoughts and emotions. For more recent figures, on the other hand, pictures and documentary film are available. Recordings may convey the voice, the cadences, even the authority of the person. Some actors immerse themselves in such research, while others may see it as an impediment to improvisation and would rather be Hamlet than JFK.

Let's not overestimate the differences between playing a historical and a fictional character. A playwright or actor may give token deference to the known facts about the historical subject, and the facts themselves may be endlessly disputed. History may be a pretext for invention and not a constraint. There are as many approaches to Richard III as Hamlet; a strong playwright like

Shakespeare turns the historical figure into a character of the imagination. Even Nixon or Elvis may be reconceived at will. An argument of postmodernists is that a so-called "real" life can be deconstructed in as many ways as a fictional one. The coherence of either is in the eye of the interpreter. But it is also possible to disagree and see the postmodern suggestion as glib, as an indulgence of skepticism little different from that of the philosopher who challenges the distinction between dream and reality.

Making "Real" Faces

When actors play Napoleon, Golda Meir, Nixon, or Elvis, there is an obvious incentive to make them look the part. The medium, as we have seen, makes a difference. On stage there is necessarily a disjunction between time and space in the play and the real time and space of the stage. Movies, by contrast, flirt with the illusion of erasing the line between staging fictional events and eavesdropping on events that are not staged. As a result, we allow stage actors greater leeway to assume roles that do not fit their appearance. A monologuist may slip into Cleopatra, Napoleon, Hitler, or Elvis with only a change of accent and posture. In movies, we generally expect the actor to look the part.

In movies, turning an actor into a historical person is a special kind of makeup problem. As with age makeups, art must conceal artifice. At the simplest level, we must be able to accept the historical figure at (literally) face value. Nothing prompts more disdain from critics than an actor embalmed in an inflexible or conspicuous prosthetic appliance.

In doing age makeups, makeup artists can capitalize on the fact that the actor must remain recognizable and that a person has the same bone structure, the same distance between the eyes, the same kind of skin and hair in youth and old age. When one turns an actor into a historical personage, however, the opposite is likely to be true. Physical characteristics vary, and it is rare to find an actor who resembles the character. (Of course, one can *cast* actors with this constraint in mind, but more often other factors—the actor's talents, availability, special interests—will trump resemblance.)

The makeup artist compromises with verisimilitude. The set of the actor's eyes, the bones of her face, her build, her posture, and her musculature are unique and typically at odds with the role. The illusion goes far beyond building up some features and giving the illusion that others are small. Countless differences must be taken into account and dealt with.

The makeup artist seems to have a choice: Get as close as possible to cloning Nixon or Mark Twain, or use caricature and give the actor the historical character's most distinctive features. Nixonian jowls, nose, and hairline may convince the audience that the actor is Nixon even if there is little actual resemblance.

In practice the choice is illusory. Caricature alone will often not work. The clues that convince us we are in the presence of Twain or Nixon may not be the obvious ones. The actor in collaboration with the makeup artist may need radical reconfiguration to imply a new shape to his face and a new way of moving. But that new appearance will inevitably and by design be a hybrid. Nothing will take him all the way to being the character's twin, and the attempt to achieve this may easily backfire.

Faces Reborn

We saw in Chapter 7 how challenges beget innovation. Aging projects drive makeup artists to find new materials and techniques, and the same is true for the re-creation of historical persons. Specialists in one kind of project—artists such as Kevin Haney, Matthew Mungle, and Gordon Smith—are also specialists in the other.

Foam latex appliances have long been the favored medium. Because turning an actor into Twain or Lincoln demands subtlety, makeup artists use multiple small appliances, carefully sculpted and finely detailed. The artist must negotiate a compromise between the actor's features and the character's, retaining as much of the actor's natural face as possible to achieve realism in movement and structure. At the same time, she must trigger the audience's recognition of the historical character, spontaneous suspension of disbelief. Embalming the actor in latex defeats both purposes.

Kevin Haney's Emmy Award–winning makeup turned Jason Robards into Mark Twain for *Mark Twain and Me* on the Disney Chan-

Figure 8.1. Jason Robards

Figure 8.2. Robards as Mark Twain in *Mark Twain and Me*. Makeup by Kevin Haney.

Figure 8.3. Kevin Haney made Robards over as Abraham Lincoln for *The Perfect Tribute*.

nel. Roughly half of Robards' face is covered by foam latex pieces, but the result is seamless, and the transformation seems complete. Skillful and daring use of many colors seals the illusion as Twain is given convincingly flush cheeks and blue-veined nose and temples.

Haney and Robards also worked together when Robards played Abraham Lincoln in *The Perfect Tribute*, an ABC television drama. Lincoln's face is bonier than Twain's, and it is fiendishly hard to mimic the gauntness and bone structure of Lincoln on an actor who lacks it. Nonetheless, Lincoln has probably been the subject of more plays and movies than any president, and Haney's work on Robards is among the more convincing attempts at resurrection.

For *Kissinger and Nixon*, a 1995 cable television drama, Haney had the opportunity to make Ron Silver over as Henry Kissinger. Again, his finesse with traditional foam latex produced a disarming tribute to the original, in equal measure cherubic and sinister. The contrast with the Lincoln makeup is in-

Figure 8.5. Another of Kevin Haney's masterworks is this rendition of Ron Silver as Henry
Kissinger in *Kissinger and Nixon*.

Figure 8.4. Ron Silver

Figure 8.6. Martin Landau

Figure 8.7. Rick Baker's acclaimed makeup turned Landau into Bela Lugosi for *Ed Wood*.

structive. Jowly lived-in faces like Kissinger's give makeup artists room to shape and experiment, room to supplement nature with rubber in ways that allow us to take the result for granted.

Among the most restrained and delicate uses of foam latex appliances is Rick Baker's transformation of Martin Landau into Bela Lugosi for his Oscar-winning performance in *Ed Wood*. Landau, tall, robust, and oval-faced is nothing like the slight, cadaverous Lugosi, whose face is an inverted triangle. And yet by widening Landau's forehead and cheekbones and using shading and color aggressively, Baker revives the essence of Lugosi—and *this* vampire withstands exposure to light.

Also notable is Jerry Quist's transformation of Robert Morse into Truman Capote. The Capote play was originally produced onstage, and the makeup was refined for the public television broadcast of the play. The makeup turns the wiry Morse into a dumpy Capote and seems to reshape the body as effectively as the face.

Figure 8.8. Robert Morse

Figures 8.9, 8.10, 8.11. Jerry Quist resurrected Truman Capote with Robert Morse as his muse, for *Capote*.

Figure 8.12. Gary Sinise

Figure 8.13. Gary Sinise became Harry Truman in his presidential years, by virtue of Gordon Smith's silicone appliances.

Figures 8.14, 8.15. The role of Bess Truman gave Diana Scarwid a chance to age, through the magic of Gordon Smith.

Other makeup artists have experimented with the new techniques that have yielded dividends in aging. Gordon Smith's finest success with silicone gel appliances has been his work on the television drama *Truman*. Gary Sinise, like Truman, is round-faced, but his features are flatter and smaller. Silicone gel appliances, unlike foam latex, work best when, masklike, they cover large surfaces. Their edges are relatively hard to blend, and in their translucency they take on the appearance of expanses of natural skin. Sinise's makeup as Truman in old age consists of two pieces that effectively cover his face, one consisting of nose and forehead, the other his lower face.

Figure 8.16. Mary Steenburgen

Smith used an even more extensive appliance to age Diana Scarwid as Bess Truman. The First Lady developed multiple chins as she aged, and Smith's reconstruction of Scarwid conveys the significant effects of gravity on Mrs. Truman's lower face and neck. Again, the makeup shows how silicone gel prosthetics mimic real skin.

A similar and equally startling effect is Gordon Smith's aging of Mary Steenburgen as Hannah Nixon for Oliver Stone's *Nixon*. Smith achieves the substantial illusion of *subtraction*, the sense that the face wearing makeup is thinner, more worn than the actress' natural appearance. The makeup also reveals a drawback of this material, the tendency to reflect light in a flatter, more uniform way than nature.

Gelatin is a different experimental material than silicone gel, less durable but even more eerily convincing as a surrogate skin. For *Ghosts of Mississippi*, Matthew Mungle turned James Woods into the elderly accused assassin of Medgar Evers, Byron de la Beckwith. Mungle saw Beckwith as a hardened, desiccated incarnation of Woods himself. The translucent prosthetic appliances, thin and pliable, are not intended to make Woods unrecognizable, and they are altogether convincing. In this sense, gelatin has both the textural advantages of silicone appliances and the seamlessness of foam latex. But it re-

Figure 8.17. Mary Steenburgen became Hannah Nixon for *Nixon*. Makeup by Gordon Smith.

mains the least resilient of the three materials, vulnerable to chemical deterioration and abrasion.

Beyond Acting

Rick Baker was one of the makeup artists, noted at the beginning of this chapter, who was asked to use his skills privately to turn a stranger into a different man. Baker turned the project down out of justified suspicion. The assumption of the strangers was obviously that, through the magic of transformational makeup, artists might turn persons into plausible versions of other persons on demand, the old *Mission: Impossible* scenario. The world would be a more interesting and treacherous place if that were so.

Figure 8.18. James Woods

The evidence available from Hollywood implies that we are far from realizing this kind of versatility in transformation. Perhaps we never will. Perhaps, as we saw in Chapter 6, techniques developed outside Hollywood for intelligence agents may have come closer to this goal than we know. But it is easy to underestimate the uniqueness of faces and the differences among them. Re-creating a Lincoln, Twain, or Nixon for movies in which lighting and camera angles can be controlled and for which scenes can be reshot stretches the present resources and the creative genius of makeup artists to their limit. The significant risk of failure makes the rare successes particularly memorable.

Figure 8.19. Woods' acclaimed performance as Byron de la Beckwith in *Ghosts of Mississippi* was mediated by Matthew Mungle's prosthetics.

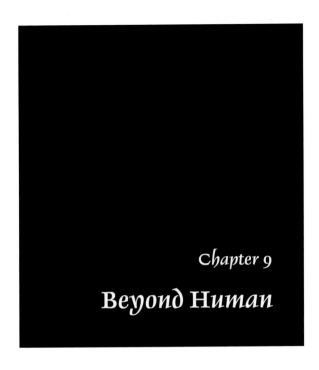

Chapter 9

Beyond Human

Know then thyself, presume not God to scan;
The proper study of mankind is Man. . . .
He hangs between, in doubt to act, or rest;
In doubt to deem himself a God or Beast. . . .
Sole judge of Truth, in endless Error hurl'd:
The glory, jest, and riddle of the World!

ALEXANDER POPE, *Essay on Man*

I do not know of any philosopher who has yet been bold enough to say,
"Here is the end which man can reach but which he can never pass."

JEAN-JACQUES ROUSSEAU, *Emile*

Learning from Clowns

The imagination is populated more richly than the world of experience. Beings and creatures not found in nature can easily be invented. We have already considered the roles of gods and demons. Gods respond to our need for order in experience, an order responsive to human concerns. We want nature to be not random but a reflection of motives, plans, and interventions of transcendent beings. Demons come into their own when gods become part of an eschatology, when our own moral sense of good and evil is projected onto the world.

Humans have always made room for more kinds of mythical beings than gods and demons. They include beasts (centaurs, unicorns, yetis), "little people" (elves, leprechauns), and even ad hoc personal facilitators (golems, genies, tooth fairies). These beings have remarkable staying power, showing up with only slight variation in many cultures. They help us define goals, explain and rationalize setbacks, and enhance our sense of power.

Among creatures of invention, clowns have a special and puzzling status. They belong to no particular myths or stories, plays, or theatrical conventions. They have their origin in commedia dell'arte, and they belong to the world of vaudeville and the circus. But clowns, like elephants and tigers, play roles outside the circus. Clowns for hire deliver singing telegrams, perform magic at children's parties, and populate parades.

The temptation to deconstruct the meaning of clowns is strong; they present clear tension between surface and subliminal meaning. The obvious mission of clowns is spontaneous fun; they meld the silliness of childhood with the slyness of ridicule, implying that adult preoccupations are never to be taken too seriously. Many clowns sort themselves out on a scale from mania to depression. Manic clowns are in constant motion, constantly topping one silly intervention with another that is more outrageous. Others mock depression; the ineffectual acts of hobo clowns are always predictably self-defeating. How can we take anything seriously if everything we do has unforeseen and explosively dire consequences?

Everyone, it is said, loves a clown. But this is hardly true. Many persons will admit that they fear and hate clowns, and there are many ways to explain why.

For one thing, to identify with clowns is perhaps, as we have seen, to identify not with fun and joy but with a form of psychological disturbance: manic hyperactivity, openly sadistic acts toward others, or morbid depression and self-absorption. The fact that clowns exaggerate and parody these states make them more, not less, troubling.

For another thing, rather than identifying with clowns we may see ourselves as their victims. Clowns mask their faces as effectively as terrorists and bank robbers. The fixed emotions caricatured on their painted faces give no clue to whatever human feelings lie beneath. Even the prosthetic faces of demons and aliens are more revealing, more accessible, since they may well reflect the wearer's emotions. Unlike characters in plays and movies, clowns are not bounded by scripts. They extemporize. In the guise of play, they seem licensed to taunt, embarrass, and coerce.

Clowns have an ambiguous status as human and not-quite-human. We do not know the rules by which they act. Their appearance justifies no expectation that they will respect the limits and deference of normal intercourse. They mock normal conventions with impunity from an undefined position that claims the prerogatives of innocent children *and* cunning adults.

A familiar theme of movies and Halloween is the diabolical and malevolent clown. Usurping a kind of power and independence, such clowns run amok. They seduce us into acquiescence.

Clowns make us think about and fear for the uncertain boundaries of what is human. We want clowns to be tethered to benign conventions of humanity, but their appearance and behavior belies those limits. We have already seen how the humanoids of science fiction and demons of horror fiction make us reconsider our assumptions about humanness. These creatures are instances of a general dilemma. Every generation redefines what it is to be human. And every generation condemns as "inhuman" patterns of conduct that turn out to be all too human.

The moral and physical dimensions of humanness cannot be separated. Ways of conceiving what is essential to our physical being are also ways of redefining our moral nature and limits. Thus the Darwinian revolution that reaffirmed our animal nature and origins seemed for troubled observers to efface the soul and human links to higher beings. Cataclysmic political events in the twentieth century have reaped that harvest as psychologists, political theorists, and philosophers have asked whether our capacities for harm and evil put us morally before or behind less reflective predators.

Other reconceptions of humanness have also taken their toll. The technology of computers and artificial intelligence has led philosophers and scientists to ask whether *our* intelligence is any different from that which we call "artificial." Do our capacities for choice, self-awareness, reflection, and self-limitation make us human, or are they illusions? We contemplate robots and computing machines and are uncertain about what we do have or *will* have in common. Increasingly we use technology to produce human beings in new ways. How long will it be before the distinction between artificially produced humans and artificial beings collapses?

In various ways makeup artists have ventured into the gray areas of humanness, the abyss between human and almost-human. Some projects bring up questions that have always troubled us, such as our ambiguous links to the world of animals. Other projects are prompted by the rapidity of change in the late twentieth century, the frequency with which persons and cultures claim to remake themselves and with which individuals turn into robots and cartoons.

Genies, Leprechauns, and Manimals

Humans need help. Among the more ubiquitous and benign myths are ones about creatures that protect us from harm, warn of danger, facilitate or grant wishes, and resolve uncertainty. Unlike us, they often know and can affect the future. While they may lack the power of gods and are often vulnerable themselves, their interventions remain, for the most part, a grace and a comfort.

But even genies, elves, and leprechauns are a mixed blessing. They can be unreliable, with a perverse will of their own. Leprechauns can take playfulness too far and play fast and loose with the interests of mere mortals. Genies are notorious for an overdeveloped sense of irony: they can give wish fulfillment a sting we cannot foresee. (Their modus operandi seems to be, "The one thing worse than not getting what you want is *getting* what you want.") Taking us both more and less seriously than we wish, they are tireless guardians of a quasi-literary sense of paradox.

If we ourselves are paradoxical, living at cross-purposes and wanting what is not in our interest, then leprechauns and genies are extensions of ourselves. They mirror our better or worse selves. As visualized in movies or TV shows, these creatures' *own* worse or better sides variously take precedence.

The movie *Leprechaun* turns the mythical fairy fickle and vengeful, the moving force in a tale of horror. But Gabe Bartalos' makeup for Warwick Davis cap-

Figure 9.1. Gabe Bartalos, pictured with Warwick Davis, turned Davis into the eponymous *Leprechaun.*

tures the ambivalence of the character more effectively than the script. Leprechauns, one hopes, are more than just another species of mindless monster.

John Dods' makeup on Carlos Lauchu for "The Gift," an episode on the TV anthology series *Monsters*, takes the opposite tack. The character is benevolent, an embodied spirit that watches over a young boy who has been kidnapped and may be killed. The immortal guardian spirit, the ghost of a Revolutionary War soldier, can change its appearance from human to animal. It communicates telepathically, and it is committed to looking after persons in grave danger. Having only limited powers, it enables the boy to avoid death only by switching identity and dying itself.

Figure 9.3. John Dods created Lauchu's magical and benign monster for an episode of *Monsters*.

Figure 9.2. Carlos Lauchu

Both Bartalos' leprechaun and Dods' Revolutionary War soldier are morally simple, if in opposite directions. In myth, genies and elves are morally complex and ambiguous, playful tricksters who toy with our characteristically human need for certainty and control. Their message is that we can gratify those needs only by paying a cost that, with hindsight, may seem too high.

Strong lessons in moral ambiguity come through comparing persons and animals. Every culture since the ancient Greeks has looked at animals symbolically; devious serpents and noble lions are cultural clichés. Astrology and Buddhist religion are among systems that use the nature of animals to give symbolic coherence to the disorder of the universe. Naturalists take up the challenge of examining these myths for factual support. Do lions and tigers, as opposed to humans, really kill only for food and not for sport or revenge? Do the genders in the animal world treat each other with more or less respect, more or less equality, than persons? What does it mean to call animals "devious"?

While philosophers and anthropologists wrestle with the puzzles of anthropomorphism, stories about "manimal" hybrids persist in collapsing the moral and physical domains. Some stories are unambiguous. Turning into a werewolf is never a capitulation to one's better nature. On the other hand, mad scientists are often inspired to improve humanity by creating human/animal hybrids. Typically they hope to borrow the strength and cunning of animals without sacrificing a moral core. Ironically the questionable morality of their very efforts shows that moral essences may be overestimated. And, predictably, their schemes backfire.

Dr. Moreau, late of *The Island of Dr. Moreau*, is second to none in hubris. H. G. Wells' novel has had three movie adaptations, variously called *The Island of Dr. Moreau* (1977 and 1996) and, appropriately, *Island of Lost Souls* (1939). The manimals in director John Frankenheimer's most recent version of *Island* were crafted by Stan Winston's makeup team. Among the creatures in rapid devolution are Lo-Mai, a leopard-man played by Mark Dacascos, and Hyena-Swine (the name speaks for itself), played by Daniel Rigney. Not quite hybrids, they are minimally human and look more like men in leopard and swine suits. Perhaps this fits the ambiguous denouement, which celebrates the triumph of anarchy over authority while suggesting that the manimals finally revert to a purely predatory state.

The lesson of Wells' *Moreau*, that of uncountable Cassandras, is that scientific ambitions may betray us, leaving us with the Frankenstein monster, the atom bomb, and global warming. The lesson is one-sided. Science also leaves us with immunizations and treatments for disease, new resources for knowledge and understanding, and the means to predict and redress natural catastrophes.

But the deeper and more specific lesson of *Moreau*, as the story has evolved, is that we are confused about the boundaries of what is human. Do we have any-

Figures 9.4, 9.5. The Hyena-Swine (played by Daniel Rigney) and Lo-Mai (the leopard-man played by Mark Dacascos) were two hybrids in the most recent version of *The Island of Dr. Moreau*. Makeup by Stan Winston Studios.

Figure 9.6. Daniel Rigney

thing to gain from the animals? Do we understand our animal nature—or even what questions to ask about it? Is our (apparently special) capacity for self-reflection, invention, and contemplation a morally ambiguous gift, one that makes possible our moral nature while also giving rise to the excesses of Dr. Moreau?

Dehumanization: Robots and Cartoons

Are we animals or machines? Both metaphors have been worked to death for much of the twentieth century. Debates about the moral implications of Darwin's revolution were already familiar a century ago. And around that time, the

Figure 9.7. Mark Dacascos

Czech writer Karel Capek coined the term "robot" to refer to machines that mimic the conduct of human beings and that might eventually replace them.

Periodically, these debates are restarted. Atrocities, both collective (World War II, Cambodia, ethnic cleansing) and individual, tend to reinvite discussion of our so-called animal nature, and some religions have never quite acquiesced in the face of evolutionary biology. The competing metaphor, man-as-machine, seems almost domesticated by the technological and theoretical changes in the last two decades. Artificial intelligence encroaches on the sinecures of "genuine" intelligence, and we are increasingly uncertain what it *cannot* do. We identify with our machines—our computers, even our cars—and see them as continuous with our selves. We seek to map the human genome, hoping to find a blueprint for persons that mirrors the structural design of machines. We are said to be on the brink of a revolution in cloning. And with increasing freedom and confidence, we substitute machines for parts of the human body and invent processes that mechanistically simulate human reproduction. We take bionics for granted.

Such movies as *Terminator 2* and the *Alien* series exploit the ease with which persons and machines will become interchangeable. Someday soon we will be hard put to distinguish real from artificial persons. Either, as science fiction has it, this will be a profound threat to humanity, or, as some philosophers suggest, the difference between persons and machines will disappear.

In fact, the very terms are already unclear. Is a machine defined by its structure, by the fact that it has mechanical rather than organic parts? If so, then many of us with surgically replaced parts are already on the way to forfeiting our humanity. Or is a machine defined by its origins, by the fact that it was produced by time-honored means of procreation? If so, then even more of us are no longer human. Or is a machine defined by its incapacity for reflection, emotion, and moral self-regard? We would like to think that this criterion suffices. But are we confident that future machines will lack these characteristics, and that present-day persons universally have them?

For the most part we are nostalgic for a clean separation of person and machine. The manlike machines of *Terminator 2* make us shudder, not only because they are relentlessly destructive but because they warn of an unknowable future. Technological advances that anticipate this future (cloning, artificial procreation, computers that mimic emotions) leave us confused by fears we cannot quite rationalize.

In 1994–1996, the Duracell company's commercials on television featured the Puttermans, characters that were popularly called "the plastic people." The Puttermans appeared to be animated by the large Duracell batteries slotted into their backs. In the ads, they enacted brief vignettes. The first series showed the Puttermans carrying out vaguely sadistic tricks on silly and boring friends who used less powerful and dependable batteries. A later series simply demonstrated the energy and resilience of the Puttermans, qualities they owed to the excellence of their batteries.

The Puttermans were robotic and stylized enough to stymie the audience. Were they animated? Were they plastic mannequins operated as puppets or as stop-motion figures? Or were they actors camouflaged by makeup? It was an open secret in the advertising community that Steve Johnson's XFX Inc. had used familiar foam latex prosthetic appliances to plasticize real actors. Lighting, backgrounds, and costumes were all manipulated to reinforce the effect. Lighting was flat, backgrounds and props were in bright and unmodulated primary colors,

Figure 9.8. Herb Putterman was patriarch of the family of robots in the familiar Duracell ads. Makeup by Steve Johnson/XFX Inc.

and costumes were made of thin vacuformed tubes and sheets of urethane-coated fabrics that shined and restricted movement.

Whatever their impact on battery sales may have been, the Puttermans reportedly did not endear themselves to their audience. Their sadism may have been a miscalculation. But a weightier concern may have been anxiety about the increasingly disputed border between persons and machines. Whether or not we welcome or tolerate machines that do our work for us and that mimic our own functions (creative or procreative), we like to keep our ontological categories clear and transparent. *Terminator 2* got it right: creatures that are ambiguously men-or-machines are to be feared. We mistrust the Puttermans for at least two reasons. Their ambiguity implies that we cannot know what to expect of them and we must be wary; their invasion of our world suggests subliminally that we are all becoming plastic.

The Puttermans could be seen as robots or cartoons. Both are animated by others: robots by their designer, cartoons by artists. We like to think that we have free will, that we are animated by no one but ourselves. Some religions posit that we are animated by transcendent beings; philosophers find the ideas of self-animation and choice endlessly tantalizing and problematic.

Movies that are adapted from cartoons borrow more than their plot. The *Batman* and *Superman* movies have villains that are marginally human. Their inherent, implacable evil seems to need no psychological explanation; the mere fact that they are cartoons seems sufficient. They have crossed from quasi-humanity into a two-dimensional world without moral parameters.

No movie conveys the menace of cartoon villains more enthusiastically than Warren Beatty's *Dick Tracy* (1990). While Tracy himself, played by Beatty, retains his human look along with human moral characteristics, the villains—Pruneface, Influence, Flattop, Mumbles, Shoulders, The Rodent and their ilk—all have grotesquely exaggerated features that echo their morally grotesque plans and values. Like objects rather than persons, they are known by descriptive labels. Doug Drexler and John Caglione Jr. won Oscars for their prosthetic make-ups, for the imagination and fidelity with which they turned actors into replicas of Chester Gould's cartoon criminals.

Unlike the world of the Puttermans, the world of *Dick Tracy* is a time, a stylized version of the 1930s, when we could distinguish comfortably between persons and subhumans/pseudohumans, between persons and machines. The certitudes of midcentury have yielded to millennial uncertainties. Faced with no crises comparable to the Great Depression or World War II, we feel free to deconstruct personhood into machines, cartoons, and disparate elements. Makeup artists are occasionally enlisted to abet our exploration of the border between persons and artificial, invented life.

Figure 9.9. R. G. Armstrong

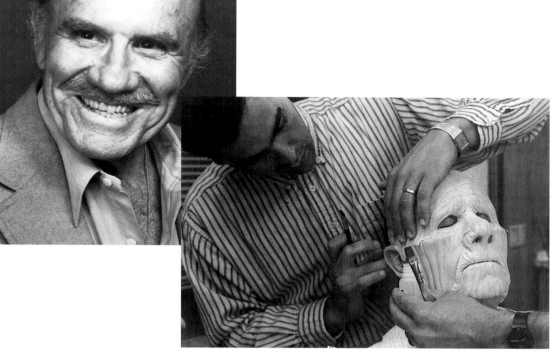

Figures 9.10, 9.11. John Caglione Jr. turned Armstrong into Pruneface, one of many living cartoons in *Dick Tracy*.

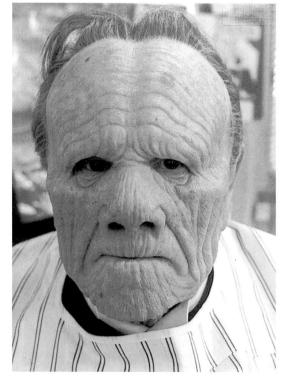

Matthew Barney:
Deconstructing Personhood

Figure 9.12. Flattop (Bill Forsythe) was another *Tracy* cartoon. Makeup by John Caglione Jr. and Doug Drexler.

Fifty years ago, critics of culture variously lamented, celebrated, or merely described a gap between so-called "high culture" and popular culture. Such talk is passé, not because there is no longer a gap but because it is no longer noteworthy. We are all more or less cultural specialists. If we know a lot about modern music, or contemporary art, or independent and foreign movies, or jazz, or modern dance, chances are that our time and attention spans are exhausted by one or two fields of interest. Only the Stephen Kings, the *Seinfeld*s, and the *Star Wars* clones have general currency.

Thus, emergent superstars in one part of our culture can be strangers to those outside. Throughout the 1990s (and his own twenties), Matthew Barney, a mixed-media New York–based artist, won national and international awards as the outstanding artist of his generation and has consistently been met with passionate, if perplexed, reviews. Critics of trendiness have called him "flavor of the month," then "flavor of the year," revised finally to the concession that he may be "flavor of the decade."

Barney's work is primarily cinematic. Over the last decade he has produced a series of increasingly elaborate and polished videos, copies of which are carefully marketed as art objects by the New York gallery that also controls stills from his videos and related sculptures and installations. His best known and most recent videos include *Drawing Restraint 7* and the current *Cremaster* series. (The cremaster muscle controls the elevation of the testicles in relation to temperature.)

More uncompromisingly than any of the works covered in this chapter, Barney demands that we reconsider what it is to be human. His courage and originality come from questioning our most familiar assumptions about human bodies and human nature, and from giving us a new visual vocabulary for struggling with these questions. The questions raised in earlier sections of this chapter were about borders: borders between man and animal, man and machine, man and cartoon. Barney takes us a few steps back and gives us images that make us question such distinctions as those between what is inside and what is outside the body, between sexuality and asexuality, between up and down (the directional effects of gravity on our bodies), and between genders.

Barney appears in many of his videos, but hardly ever in his natural guise. Using the makeup talents of Gabe Bartalos, he inhabits beings that ambiguously cross persons and animals, persons and gods, persons and mythical beings. In *Drawing Restraint 7* he becomes a satyr, but clearly a novice, a young buck. His satyr lacks horns, unlike the two well-muscled, well-antlered satyrs that wrestle for dominance in much of the video. In *Cremaster 4* he presents himself again as a kind of ram (called the Loughton Candidate), again with horns that have yet to emerge but this time dressed in the white suit of a vaudeville entertainer and devoid of obvious mythological reference. Most recently, in *Cremaster 5*, he plays three figures—the Diva, the Magician, and the Giant. While the androgynous Diva and the heroic Magician are largely human, the Giant is a demigod whose body flowers from exotic aquatic plants.

Figure 9.13. Matthew Barney became a young satyr for *Drawing Restraint 7*. Makeup by Gabe Bartalos/Atlantic West Effects.

Figure 9.14. A pair of mature satyrs from *Drawing Restraint 7.* Makeup by Gabe Bartalos/Atlantic West Effects.

The use of makeup to transform Barney's body is at least as significant as his facial appliances. In *Drawing Restraint 7* and *Cremaster 5* he notably lacks sexual organs. In both videos his lower legs are also transformed, in *DR7* into the hind quarters of a goat and in *C5* into the leaves of the luxuriant plants from which his character apparently flowers. Moreover, his body in each video is hairless and covered with body paint that makes it appear unnaturally translucent and pale.

In itself, Barney's use of makeup is no more or less imaginative and skillful than many other projects we have examined. But it plays a tantalizing role in his re-examination of human nature. For one thing, the asexuality of his incarnations are not simply sexual ambiguity or androgyny. Disputes over whether his art has a gay or straight orientation are beside the point. The realm of experience to which he draws us is presexual, the stage of discovering that one is a discrete being capable of exploring himself and his world. In an interview, Barney remarked that the eroticism of his work is autoeroticism.

In *Drawing Restraint 7*, a limousine speeding through the tunnels of New York City contains in the back seats two mature satyrs, mirror images of each other, wrestling in a sexualized fight to death. In the front frolics an immature, unhorned satyr (Barney), who explores his domain, gradually entangling himself with the car's deconstructed interior. Perhaps they are stages of the same ambiguous creature—not quite sexualized, not quite human—at war with himself as an adult, at pains to know and distinguish himself from his environment as an adolescent.

In *Cremaster 4*, Barney's now clothed (white-suited) satyr tapdances at the end of a pier, then slips into the water through a hole, fighting his way back to land by climbing through a dense (alimentary?) tunnel made of a pale, viscous substance. In *Cremaster 5*, the Magician plunges to his watery death, chained and Houdini-like, from a bridge in Budapest, and the acrobatic Diva climbs a flowering vine from which he falls and dangles.

 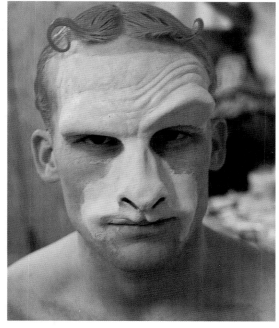

Figures 9.15, 9.16. Bartalos' prosthetics turn Matthew Barney into the Loughton Candidate for *Cremaster 4*.

Figure 9.17. The Loughton Candidate dances. Makeup by Gabe Bartalos/Atlantic West Effects.

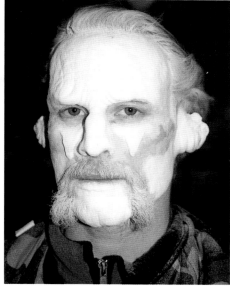

Figures 9.18, 9.19, 9.20.
The Giant in *Cremaster 5*
is part plant, part human.
Gabe Bartalos' makeup
again transforms
Matthew Barney.

In one of Barney's early, less ornately decorated videos he explores a gymnasium naked except for a harness. He climbs laboriously toward the ceiling, from which he repeatedly falls, eventually impaling himself. In another early video he obsessively devotes himself to (apparently) sealing the body's orifices. In both videos the same substance that lines the *Cremaster 4* tunnel, one that suggests petroleum jelly or tapioca and that observers compare to paste, sperm, or the lining of body cavities, is ubiquitous, used variously to (de)construct gymnasium equipment and to close the body's openings.

It is possible to find many meanings (or none) in Barney's enigmatic works—and they are conspicuously easy to ridicule. While art journals pay him (and his talent for winning awards) awestruck if somewhat grudging deference, reviews in the daily newspapers, the *New York Times* for example, call him "vaguely prurient," "ridiculously solemn," and "bogus." And yet he seems to have the staying power of an entertainer who is consistently original and stirs the imagination.

Aside from the themes of pre-sexuality and an aggressively athletic and solitary exploration of body and environment, he leads us to rethink elementary pairings. In his images we are often simultaneously inside and outside the body, inside and outside suggestive containers. Tunnels and cars both surround us and exist to be explored. Admitting no light, sometimes made up of blubbery substances, they mimic the tunnels of our bodies. Our explorations cause us to rise and fall in ways out of our control, just as the cremaster muscle raises and lowers the testicles in relation only to ambient temperature. Yet another idea is that the mysterious substance of our immediate environment is neither liquid nor solid but in between, neither colored nor colorless but in between. It is immediate to us but permanently eludes our grasp—physically and conceptually.

Barney's videos are full of other events and elements. Their tone is playful, and yet their structure is rigorous. Is their symbolism a tease? Arguably not. Teasing suggests that Barney has a demonstrable code in mind, one that is tantalizingly hidden. I suspect that, like other interesting artists, what he wants to tell us is manifest in his work and no code is likely to help explain it. We stumble if we try to translate it into words or otherwise familiar symbols since he is playing with a new iconography.

What seems clear is that his transformations echo and transcend the distinctions in this chapter—person and machine, real and artificial person, real person and mythical being, person and cartoon. If he is right, we are more confused than ever about what is human.

From Identity to Humanity

Playing God, makeup artists give actors—give us—new identities. From one standpoint, these transformations remain mere pretense and artifice. Actors in disguise, as aliens, as historical figures, or as monsters are all playing parts, usually one that is scripted and predetermined. For the most part no one is really fooled, not fellow actors, not movie and TV audiences. In a matter of hours familiar identities, ordinary faces, are restored.

From another point of view, all this is wrong. Familiar identities are ones that we make up as we go along. We have misgivings about whether the self we know is the self that others see. The illusory comfort that we get from consistency is offset by the fantasy of being recreated, transformed, unfamiliar. In that sense, the makeup artist taps into a seductive, dangerous, and perhaps universal need. The actor transformed realizes a new possibility of himself, a new being that both is and is not himself. To leave the makeup behind is not just to be restored, but to be diminished.

Some of the most intriguing makeup projects take us from individual to collective identity. They put in play questions about humanity as well as identity. And they make us reflect how uncertain we are about what is distinctively human.

Afterthoughts

> How can [the gods] meet us face to face till we have faces?
>
> C. S. LEWIS, *Till We Have Faces*

More than most persons, philosophers are in the business of reminding us of the obvious—and finding it peculiarly interesting. It is obvious that other people are the objects of our thoughts and feelings much of the time. And we tend to identify other people with their faces. Not only do we recognize them by their faces, but we think of their faces as reflecting or concealing whatever lies behind.

When we look at other persons, their faces alone are both public and natural (part of nature). Bodies are natural, but generally not publicly visible; clothes are visible but not natural. Faces, natural faces, give us access to others.

The simulation of faces is, therefore, a strange and disconcerting art. The possibility of perfect simulation, counterfeit faces unrecognizable as such, threatens everyday assumptions about our lives and relationships. Fortunately, face creation is difficult and exacting, and it is mostly limited to discrete contexts like moviemaking.

Even if the contexts are limited, the fantasies to which they give rise are not. They express both the carnival fantasy of concealment and disguise as well as the wish to know ourselves at other ages and in other conditions. Provisionally they give us the means to become great or notorious persons in history. They allow us to envision possibilities beyond the human and the known: aliens, the demonic, and human hybrids of indefinitely many kinds.

The art of transformational makeup is subversive. Its goal is often to erase the distinction between the real and the artificial. More distinctively than other arts, it tries to cover its own tracks. The audience is expected to take the invented person at, literally, face value. For the actor it is also subversive, subtracting the dimension of recognition by others and, sometimes, even by himself.

Self-knowledge, it might be said, is hard enough even if we discount the possibility of imposture, of becoming other selves. Our real selves are complex and contradictory even if we ignore the selves we take on as pretense. But perhaps the opposite is true. Perhaps we only know ourselves when we take account of our fantasies and possible selves. Perhaps we are the sum of our imaginings.

Photo Credits

Figures 4.1, 4.2, 4.3, 4.4. Photos used with permission of Howard Berger/KNB Studios.

Figure 4.5. Photo used with permission of Walter Phelan.

Figure 4.6. Photo used with permission of Josh Patton.

Figure 4.7. Photo used with permission of Walter Phelan, Josh Patton, and Todd Masters/MastersFX.

Figures 4.8, 4.9, 4.10, 4.11, 4.12, 4.13. Photos used with permission of John Vulich/Optic Nerve and Todd McIntosh.

Figure 4.14. Photo used with permission of Mark Metcalf.

Figure 4.15. Photo used with permission of John Vulich/Optic Nerve and Todd McIntosh.

Figure 4.16. Photo used with permission of Toby Lindala.

Figure 4.17. Photo used with permission of Vincent D'Onofrio.

Figure 4.18. Photo used with permission of Rick Baker/Cinovation Studios and Vincent D'Onofrio.

Figure 4.19. Photo used with permission of Alan Shockley-Gray.

Figure 4.20. Photo used with permission of Steve Johnson/XFX Inc. and Alan Shockley-Gray.

Figure 4.21. Photo used with permission of T. Ryder Smith.

Figure 4.22. Photo used with permission of Steve Johnson/XFX Inc. and T. Ryder Smith.

Figure 4.23. Photo used with permission of Steve Johnson/XFX Inc.

Figures 4.24, 4.25, 4.26, 4.27. Photos used with permission of Todd McIntosh.

Figure 4.28. Photo used with permission of Brian Blair.

Figure 4.29. Photo used with permission of John Vulich/Optic Nerve and Brian Blair.

Figures 4.30, 4.31, 4.32, 4.33, 4.34. Photos used with permission of Gabe Bartalos/Atlantic West Effects.

Figure 4.35. Photo used with permission of Chris Norris.

Figure 4.36. Photo used with permission of Toby Lindala and Chris Norris.

Figure 4.37. Photo used with permission of Jonathan Fuller.

Figures 4.38, 4.39, 4.40, 4.41, 4.42. Photos used with permission of John Vulich/Optic Nerve and Jonathan Fuller.

Figures 5.1, 5.2. *Star Trek VI* © 2000 by Paramount Pictures. All Rights Reserved.

Figures 5.3, 5.4, 5.5, 5.6. *Star Trek: Deep Space Nine* © 2000 by Paramount Pictures. All Rights Reserved.

Figure 5.7. Photo used with permission of Eric Pierpoint.

Figure 5.8. Photo used with permission of Richard Snell and Eric Pierpoint.

All characters from *Babylon 5* are the property of Warner Bros. Studios. No infringement is intended. Their use in this book is for informational and analytical purposes only.

Figures 5.9, 5.10, 5.11, 5.12, 5.13, 5.14, 5.15, 5.16, 5.17, 5.18, 5.19. Photos used with permission of John Vulich/Optic Nerve.

Figure 5.20. Photo used with permission of Kim Strauss.

Figures 5.21, 5.22, 5.23, 5.24. Photos used with permission of John Vulich/Optic Nerve and Kim Strauss.

Figure 5.25. Photo used with permission of Michael McKenzie.

Figures 5.26, 5.27, 5.28, 5.29. Photos used with permission of John Vulich/Optic Nerve and Michael McKenzie.

Figure 5.30. Photo used with permission of Wayne Alexander.

Figure 5.31. Photo used with permission of John Vulich/Optic Nerve and Wayne Alexander.

Figures 5.32, 5.33. Photos used with permission of John Vulich/Optic Nerve.

Figure 5.34. Photo used with permission of Tim Choate.

Figures 5.35, 5.36. Photos used with permission of John Vulich/Optic Nerve and Tim Choate.

Figure 5.37. Photo used with permission of Eric Zivot.

Figure 5.38. Photo used with permission of John Vulich/Optic Nerve and Eric Zivot.

Figure 5.39. Photo used with permission of Josh Patton.

Figure 5.40. Photo used with permission of John Vulich/Optic Nerve and Josh Patton.

Figure 5.41. Photo used with permission of Todd Masters/MastersFX and Josh Patton.

Figure 5.42. Photo used with permission of Walter Phelan.

Figures 5.43, 5.44. Photos used with permission of John Vulich/Optic Nerve and Walter Phelan.

Figures 5.45, 5.46, 5.47, 5.48, 5.49, 5.50. Photos used with permission of John Vulich/Optic Nerve.

Figure 6.1. Photo used with permission of Dennis Christopher.

Figure 6.2. Photo used with permission of Todd Masters/MastersFX and Dennis Christopher.

Figures 6.3, 6.4, 6.5. Photos used with permission of Norman Bryn.

Figure 6.6. Photo used with permission of Anthony LaPaglia.

Figures 6.7, 6.8, 6.9, 6.10. Photos used with permission of Kevin Haney and Anthony LaPaglia.

Figure 6.11. Photo used with permission of Charlie Sheen.

Figure 6.12. Photo used with permission of Todd Masters/MastersFX and Charlie Sheen.

Figures 6.13, 6.14, 6.15, 6.16, 6.17. Photos used with permission of Steve Johnson/XFX Inc.

Figure 6.18. Photo used with permission of Christopher Plummer.

Figures 6.19, 6.20. Photos used with permission of Carl Fullerton and Christopher Plummer.

Figures 6.21, 6.22, 6.23, 6.24. *Coming to America* © 2000 by Paramount Pictures. All Rights Reserved.

Figures 6.25, 6.26, 6.27, 6.28, 6.29. *The Nutty Professor* © 1997 by Universal Studios, Inc. All Rights Reserved.

Figures 6.30, 6.31, 6.32, 6.33, 6.34. Photos used with permission of Kevin Yagher.

Figures 6.35, 6.36, 6.37, 6.38, 6.39. Photos used with permission of Steve Johnson/XFX Inc.

Figures 6.40, 6.41. Photos used with permission of Göran Lundström/Effects Studio (Stockholm). Photos appear courtesy of Bjorn Edergen/SVT.

Figure 6.42. Photo used with permission of Göran Lundström/Effects Studio (Stockholm). Photo appears courtesy of Effects Studio.

Figures 7.1, 7.2. *Star Trek: Deep Space Nine* © 2000 by Paramount Pictures. All Rights Reserved.

Figures 7.3, 7.4, 7.5, 7.6, 7.7. Photos used with permission of Norman Bryn.

Figures 7.8, 7.9. Photo used with permission of Todd McIntosh.

Figures 7.10, 7.11. Photos used with permission of Greg Funk and Fionagh Cush.

Figure 7.12. Photo used with permission of D. B. Sweeney.

Figure 7.13. Photo used with permission of Todd Masters/MastersFX and D. B. Sweeney.

Figure 7.14. Photo used with permission of Travis Tritt.

Figure 7.15. Photo used with permission of Todd Masters/MastersFX and Travis Tritt.

Figure 7.16. Photo used with permission of Eric Close.

Figure 7.17. Photo used with permission of Todd Masters/MastersFX and Eric Close.

Figures 7.18, 7.19. Photos used with permission of Todd Masters/MastersFX.

Figure 7.20. Photo used with permission of Keith Szarabajka.

Figure 7.21. Photo used with permission of Carl Fullerton and Keith Szarabajka.

Figures 7.22, 7.23. Photos used with permission of Gordon Smith/FXSmith.

Figures 7.24, 7.25. Photos used with permission of Pierre-Olivier Thévènin and Almost Human Studios.

Figures 7.26, 7.27, 7.28, 7.29. Photos used with permission of Matthew Mungle.

Figure 7.30. Photo used with permission of Richard Dean Anderson.

Figures 7.31, 7.32. Photos used with permission of Steve Johnson/XFX Inc. and Richard Dean Anderson.

Figures 7.33, 7.34, 7.35, 7.36. Photos used with permission of Tim Allen and Barry Koper.

Figures 7.37, 7.38. Photos used with permission of ADI/Alec Gillis and Tom Woodruff Jr.

Figures 7.39, 7.40. Photos used with permission of Tim Allen and Barry Koper.

Figure 7.41. Photo used with permission of ADI/Alec Gillis and Tom Woodruff Jr.

Figure 7.42. Photo used with permission of Tim Allen and Barry Koper.

Figures 7.43, 7.44, 7.45. Photos used with permission of Kevin Haney and Alan Cumming.

Figure 7.46. Photo used with permission of Michael Biehn.

Figures 7.47, 7.48. Photos used with permission of Michèle Burke and Michael Biehn.

Figure 8.1. Photo used with permission of Jason Robards.

Figures 8.2, 8.3. Photos used with permission of Kevin Haney and Jason Robards.

Figure 8.4. Photo used with permission of Ron Silver.

Figure 8.5. Photo used with permission of Kevin Haney and Ron Silver.

Figure 8.6. Photo used with permission of Martin Landau.

Figure 8.7. Photo used with permission of Rick Baker/Cinovation Studios and Martin Landau.

Figure 8.8. Photo used with permission of Robert Morse.

Figures 8.9, 8.10, 8.11. Photos used with permission of Gerald Quist and Robert Morse.

Figure 8.12. Photo used with permission of Gary Sinise.

Figures 8.13, 8.14. Photos used with permission of Gordon Smith/FXSmith and Gary Sinise.

Figure 8.15. Photo used with permission of Gordon Smith/FXSmith.

Figure 8.16. Photo used with permission of Mary Steenburgen.

Figure 8.17. Photo used with permission of Gordon Smith/FXSmith and Mary Steenburgen.

Figure 8.18. Photo used with permission of James Woods.

Figure 8.19. Photo used with permission of Matthew Mungle and James Woods.

Figure 9.1. Photo used with permission of Gabe Bartalos/Atlantic West Effects.

Figures 9.2, 9.3. Photos used with permission of John Dods.

Figures 9.4, 9.5. *The Island of Dr. Moreau* © 1996 New Line Productions, Inc. All rights reserved. Photos appear courtesy of New Line Productions, Inc.

Figure 9.6. Photo used with permission of Mike Smithson.

Figure 9.7. Photo used with permission of Mark Dacascos.

Figure 9.8. Photo used with permission of Steve Johnson/XFX Inc. and Duracell, U.S.A.

Figure 9.9. Photo used with permission of R. G. Armstrong.

Figures 9.10, 9.11, 9.12. Photos used with permission of John Caglione Jr.

Figure 9.13. Matthew Barney, *Drawing Restraint* 7, 1993. © 1993 Matthew Barney. Production still. Production: Michael James O'Brien. Courtesy Barbara Gladstone.

Figure 9.14. Matthew Barney, *Drawing Restraint* 7, 1993. Spin Track. © 1993 Matthew Barney. Video still. Videography: Peter Strietmann. Courtesy Barbara Gladstone.

Figures 9.15, 9.16. Photo used with permission of Matthew Barney and Gabe Bartalos/Atlantic West Effects.

Figure 9.17. Matthew Barney, *Cremaster* 4, 1994. © 1994 Matthew Barney. Production still. Photography: Michael James O'Brien. Courtesy Barbara Gladstone.

Figures 9.18, 9.19. Photos used with permission of Matthew Barney and Gabe Bartalos/Atlantic West Effects.

Figure 9.20. Matthew Barney, *Cremaster* 5, 1997. © 1997 Matthew Barney. Production still. Photo credit: Michael James O'Brien. Courtesy Barbara Gladstone.

Index

Judaism, ancient, 49
Jumanji, 147
Jung, Carl, 13
Jupiter, 5
Jurasik, Peter, 96, 97

Kandinsky, Wassily, 32
Katsulis, Andreas, *100*
Keats, John, 32
Kennedy, John F. (Jack), 36, 188
Kerns, Joanna, 165, 168, *169*
Khan, Genghis, 153
Kind Hearts and Coronets (1949), 140, 142
King, Stephen, 136, 138, 168, 170, 214
Kissinger, Henry, 192, *193*, 194
Kissinger and Nixon, 192, *193*
KNB Studios, 9, 38, 53, 54, 55
Koper, Barry, *178*, *179*, 180, *181*
Kurtzman, Bob, 53

Lalitavistara, 50, 51
Lancaster, Burt, 125
Landau, Martin, *194*
LaPaglia, Anthony, *131*, *132*, *133*, 144
Lauchu, Carlos, 206
Legends of the Fall, 170
    characters: Ludlow, Alfred, 170; Ludlow,
        Tristan, 170; One Stab, 170, *172*
Lenin, 187
Leone, Sergio, 84
Leprechaun, 205
Leprechauns, 205, 207
Les Jeux et Les Hommes, 24
Leung, Tony, 171, *174*, 176
Lewis, Juliette, 53
Lily in Love (1985), 138, *139*
Lincoln, Abraham, 6, 8, 21, 165, 187, 188,
    190, *192*, 200
Lindala, Toby, 62, 72, 73
List of Adrian Messenger, The (1963), 37, 125,
    126, 141
Little Big Man, 34, 37, 159
    character: Crabb, Jack, 159
Lost Boys, The, 64, 65, 66
Lucifer, 49, 51
Lugosi, Bela, *194*
Lundström, Göran (Effects Studio), 150, *151*,
    152, 153

Makeup artists
    education and background of, 36–40
    work, nature of, 7–11
Manicheanism, 51
Manimals, 206–208
Man Who Fell to Earth, The, 84, 85
Mardi Gras, 24, 26
Mark Twain and Me, 190, *191*
Martinpelto, Jenny, *151*
Martz, Neal, 170

Mask, The, 79
Masks, 40, 123
    theatrical use of, 122–125
Masquerade festivals, 24–27
    Carnival, 24
    Halloween, 24–27, 33, 204
    Mardi Gras, 24, 26
Masters, Todd (MastersFX), 9, 38, 56, 57, 113,
    128, 129, 134, 135, 165, 166, 167, 168,
    169, 176
McDonald, Philip, 125
McIntosh, Todd, 56, 59, 67, 68, *163*, 165
McKenzie, Michael, *104*, *105*
Meir, Golda, 189
Melies, Georges, 85
Mendez, Antonio, 150, 153
Men in Black, 38, 63, 65
Mephistopheles, 49, 60
Merchant of Venice, The, 123
Merlin, Jan, 126
Metcalf, Mark, *60*, *61*
Michelangelo, 21, 32, 49
Mission: Impossible, 134, 153, 186, 187, 199
Mitchum, Robert, 125
Moby Dick, 60
Molnar, Ferenc, 138
Monsters, 206
Morgan, Darin, 62, 65
Morot, Adrien, *136*, *137*
Morse, Robert, *195*
Mortality, 15–16
    See also immortality
Mother Teresa, 21
Møystad, Erik, *151*, *152*
Mozart, 32
Mungle, Matthew, 9, 34, 39, *157*, 171, *174*,
    175, 176, 178, 190, 198, 201
Murphy, Eddie, 9, 34, 41, 79, 119, *140*, *141*,
    142, *143*, 144, 153, 178

Nicotero, Greg, 9, 38, 53
Night of the Living Dead, 71
Nimoy, Leonard, 87
1984, 81
Nixon, 188, 198, *199*
Nixon, Hannah, 198, *199*
Nixon, Richard, 19, 42, 78, 187, 189, 190, 200
Norris, Chris Nelson, 73
Norse mythology, 121
    character: Loki, 121
Nutty Professor, The, 9, 34, 38, 41, 79, 119,
    140, 142, 144
    characters: Klump, Ernie (brother), 34, *143*;
        Father Klump, *144*; Grandmother Klump,
        143; Mother Klump, 34, *144*; Klump,
        Sherman, 142, *143*, 178; the Klumps, 41,
        142; Love, Buddy, 178; Simmons,
        Richard, 142